Puppy
in the
Pulpit

Raelene Phillips

Raelene Phillips

Evergreen
PRESS

Puppy in the Pulpit
by Raelene Phillips
Copyright ©2003 Raelene Phillips

ISBN 1-58169-125-4
For Worldwide Distribution
Printed in the U.S.A.

Fifth printing, August 2005

Evergreen Press
P.O. Box 191540 • Mobile, AL 36619

Table of Contents

Dedication

This book is lovingly dedicated to the memory
of my first beloved pet:

Tippy Wood
1959-1969

She was the first to show me the unconditional
love a dog gives to her family. I am grateful.

I would also like to dedicate this book to my
two special nieces—Joann and Sara Wood.

They are also Dixie's friends! May God bless
you both as you have blessed me.

Acknowledgments

I thank God for so many people who have encouraged me on this project:

First, I thank my wonderful husband, Danny, for listening to each chapter as I wrote them and for suggestions which made the manuscript better. I thank our children, Sonya and Kyer, for allowing me to share some of their stories. I hope you are not too surprised!

My brothers, Bill, Bob, Johnny, and David—I suppose all your teasing helped to mold me into the person I am today. I'm grateful to have grown up with the knowledge that the four of you were always there when I needed you.

I owe a debt of gratitude to the late Mrs. Caroline Brennamen who taught me everything I know about writing in her Junior American Literature English class. She graded fairly and challenged me to be the best I could be.

I also must thank everyone at C.L.A.S.S. (Christian Leaders Authors and Speakers Services). Florence Littauer is inspiring. Marita Littauer is hilariously encouraging. And Craig Sundheimer helped me to design the brochure about myself as a speaker which started this whole ball rolling. I owe you one, Craig!

At Evergreen Press, Keith Carroll has led me through the publication process step-by-step. He has been very patient and I am grateful. Thanks also to Kathy Banashak for the fine job she did of editing. While phone calls and e-mails have been nice, I look forward to meeting both of you in person.

Joyce Buetner, my biggest cheerleader, thanks again. All the times I have come to Elida Middle School to share in your classes have been so much fun. Some day that condo in Hawaii might become a reality!

Margaret Hossler, Dorothy Day, Eleanor Hatfield, Nadine Steele, Chris Fifer, Barb Shepherd, Dortha Bice, Monyeen Boyed, and especially Mom—all women friends who give me love, joy, and so much encouragement. May God give back to you as you have given to me.

To the people of Newson Missionary Church on Cowpath Road in rural Champaign County, Ohio— thanks for your love and acceptance of this city-kid pastor's wife. And, thanks for allowing a dog in the parsonage.

Last (but definitely not least)—a huge debt of gratitude to Dixie Lee!

Introduction

If I could ever afford to own an original oil painting, I know which painting I would want to purchase. It was painted by Francis Barraud in 1898 and is titled, "His Master's Voice." If you do not recognize the name of the painting, I can almost guarantee that you would recognize the actual masterpiece. On the left of the painting is an antique gramophone, which is a very early version of a record player. The gramophone had a crank on the side. You placed a record (like a very large CD) on a turntable and cranked the handle to make it play. Coming from the top of the turntable was a large bell-shaped speaker that almost looked like the bell of a trumpet. The music was directed into this bell and the sound was broadcast through it. On the right side of the painting is a beautiful dog that is looking into the bell of the gramophone with his head cocked to the left. You can tell the dog is listening intently and is a bit confused.

When asked about his painting back in 1898, Mr. Barraud is reported to have said that the dog's name was Nipper. He was aptly named because he had a terrible habit of nipping at people's heels. Nipper's master had made a recording of himself speaking, which he played on the gramophone. The painter watched as the dog owner played the recording of his voice. Nipper ran to the gramophone and stared into the bell shaped speaker. Mr. Barraud said he noticed "how puzzled he was to make out where the voice came from," tipping his head from side to side.

Evidently this whole scene made quite an impression on Francis Barraud. Nipper (who was a black and white terrier mix) lived happily for eleven years, from 1884 to 1895. Three years later Mr. Barraud could not get the scene of Nipper and the gramophone out of his mind, so he painted what was to become one of the most famous doggy paintings of all times.

If you have never seen the painting, look on the front of older models of stereos or televisions made by RCA Victor. "His Master's Voice" became their logo in the early 1900s. The reason, I suppose, is obvious. If the recording sounded so clear that it would cause a dog to drop whatever it was doing and run to listen, it meant that the record player had good quality sound. The advertising executives at RCA Victor knew a good thing when they saw it!

I have never worked for RCA or even had a gramophone in my house. I also never had a terrier mix dog that looked anything like the dog in the painting. Why, then, the reader might ask, would I want to own that famous painting? The answer to that question is simple. The painting always makes me think of my relationship with God.

The late Gilda Radner once said, "Dogs are the most amazing creatures; they give unconditional love. For me they are the role model for being alive." I could not agree more wholeheartedly with Ms. Radner's statement.

As she said, dogs *do* give unconditional love. We had a little poodle one time that had been badly abused. We had been looking for a non-shedding variety of dog (due to our daughter's allergies), but doubted we could afford to purchase one. I read through the dog advertisements in our newspaper every evening, hoping to find one. Imagine my surprise when there was an ad for a "free poodle!" I was on the phone immediately and went to see the dog in spite of my misgivings.

The lady on the phone had said, "Oh, yeah. We have a dumb little mutt that's out in our barn. We jist want to give it away 'cause it's useless. It jist gits in the way when my husband is out thar. It cain't even kill a mouse."

Upon arrival at the barn, the farmer kicked a little furball in our direction. I picked up a cowering, tiny, apricot-colored poodle that looked like it had never been clipped or brushed. You could barely see its little face. I didn't even know if it had a name or how old it was. I was so outraged at the treatment this little pup had been given that I immediately said, "We will take her home."

We dubbed the pathetic creature "Suzie." The vet estimated that she was probably eight or ten years old. Wouldn't you think that after being so badly abused for such a long time she would have been wary to allow herself to love again? Wouldn't you think she would have avoided people's feet like a plague, if she had been kicked around a barn her entire life? Suzie, however, was a different kind of dog. She was sweet and lovable and became friends with everyone she met. She only lived a couple years with us, but they were happy years. What always amazed me about Suzie was remembering that first time we saw her. When the farmer, who obviously hated this dog, whistled for her to come to him, she trotted toward him with tail wagging, and he kicked her away! I don't know many people who love so unconditionally that even after being kicked many times they would still "wag their tails" and come when called. But that's the way God loves the world.

We recently took our dog, Dixie, to have her picture taken. The store where we purchased her was running a special promotion for Easter. They brought in a professional photographer with all the fancy lighting, backgrounds, and all sorts of props. The make-shift studio looked exactly like I remembered real photography studios looking when we took our children for pictures when they were small. And so, the photo shoot began.

We tried to get Dixie to sit in a little chair, which we accomplished by placing her favorite teddy bear in the chair with her, putting her leash through the wicker and holding on tight. The photographer had to work fast, for the store was full of all sorts of animals and intriguing displays that vied for the dog's attention.

The photographer had an assistant whose job it was to get the dog to look at the right place. The assistant had all sorts of toys: one plastic dog squeaked, one thing rattled, and another rang a bell when she shook it. She even played a tiny harmonica. This poor lady was bouncing all over the place while the photographer merrily snapped pictures. We soon discovered, however, that there was a much better way to get Dixie's attention. She responded much more quickly to my husband Dan's voice than she did to any of the assistant's bells and whistles. Dan calmly stood behind the photographer and called her name. She would tilt her head at much the same angle that the ancient Nipper did in the painting. Her master's voice calmed her anxious spirit. The pictures were wonderful!

When I look at a print of Francis Barraud's painting, but more importantly, when I look at our beloved Dixie Lee, I am reminded that I have a Master in heaven who is always talking to me. When I get my mind off all the other "animals" and all the "toys" and noisy things in my life, and listen only to His voice—it is then that I find peace.

It is my hope that as you read this book, you can "get away from it all" for a short length of time. Allow your mind to wander back and remember every pet you ever had. If you currently share your life with a wonderful four-footed friend, pat your lap and allow him or her to share the chair with you. If they want to lick or chew the edge of the page, just this once say "Go for it." As you read and contemplate your pet friends, check to see if there is another "Voice" that would like for you to listen.

Happy reading!

—*Raelene Phillips*

"God loves you, and so do I!"
—*Dixie Lee*

1

The Choice

My friend and I laughed at the antics of the two bulldog puppies wrestling in the shredded paper display of the pet store window. Eleanor had recently moved into a lovely new home in a retirement community, changing her life pretty dramatically. Thinking that she seemed a bit lonely, I had been trying valiantly to talk her into getting a four-legged friend of the canine variety to share her life, so I was pleased when she took me by the arm and said, "Let's go inside."

She told me how she thought the cutest dogs were the little tiny collies called shelties, but she had never had a dog as a pet before. Fancying myself a bit of an expert in dog breeds, I proceeded to give her the plusses and minuses of all the various kinds of dogs with which I was familiar. I was about to say that shelties are notoriously very protective and "one person" type dogs, when I saw a darling little bundle of fur sitting atop a tiny pillow in the fifth cage. My eyes filled with tears, and I couldn't believe how much she looked just like "Rebel," our schnauzer who had died of a mysterious, undiagnosed disease two years earlier.

Eleanor turned to tell me that she couldn't find any of the little collies when she saw the look on my face. One glimpse of the gray puppy had turned me into a blubbering bowl of mush. Following my gaze, she immediately exclaimed, "Oh! It's adorable!"

The saleslady had astutely stood back to watch this interchange and slowly approached us to ask, "Can I get one of the puppies out for you ladies to play with?"

Quickly swiping my hand across my leaking eyes, I said, "No. We were hoping to find a sheltie, but it looks as though you don't have any." My eyes never left cage #5 as I spoke.

Eleanor asked, "How much is that little schnauzer?"

The saleslady (who I am sure was watching my face) immediately went into her full sales pitch. "Oh, isn't she the cutest little thing you ever saw? But, she's not technically a schnauzer; she's a schnoodle. Her mother was a full-blooded toy poodle, and her father was a full-blooded miniature schnauzer. The puppies are getting so popular. They have all the good traits of both of the breeds. Some people think this will be the next breed to be recognized by the AKC. Here, let me get her out for you."

"No!" I choked. Turning to Eleanor I said,

"Unless *you* have changed your mind. I thought you wanted a sheltie."

Eleanor can read my mind like a modern day Sigmund Freud. "Let's play with it. You know you need another dog. You can't mourn Rebel forever."

Shaking my head, I stood firm. Pulling Eleanor by the arm, I decided it was time to hit the sales at the department store further down the mall. Two outfits per person and much less money in our purses later, we were headed to the car.

"Let's go look at the schnoodle again," my friend pleaded.

I think the saleslady had been standing at the doorway watching for us. We were no more than inside the glass doors when she placed this wriggling little chunk of fur into my arms. The puppy immediately licked me right on the mouth, much to Eleanor's delight.

"Puppy breath!" I giggled.

Knowing me better than I know myself, Eleanor responded, "I would have been disappointed if you hadn't said that!" And we were on our way to the fenced in area where prospective buyers are encouraged to play with the pups.

I am convinced that if "puppy breath" could be put into a bottle there would be a large market to sell it as a perfume or room freshener. I know that I would purchase it by the caseload because to me it smells like love! I suppose only true dog lovers know what I mean. One whiff reduces me to a babbling idiot. And this little schnoodle seemed to want to pant all over my face.

As we sat on the tiny little stools in the oversized playpen, I think Eleanor felt foolish. She took my purse and shopping bags and placed them atop hers in the corner. Meanwhile, though I had worn a skirt and blouse outfit complete with hose and good shoes (for trying on outfits), I sprawled on the floor and played tug of war with the little pup.

"BF (our code for each other: Best Friend), I know you think you want a sheltie, but this dog has personality. And she's smart. Look at her fetch the ball," I said.

"She *is* adorable, but we're not here for me, BF. You need this dog!" Eleanor responded.

Surprised, I looked up to see a nodding head. She began to explain that she had changed her mind and didn't think she wanted to try and housebreak a pup. "But you're so good at it. And you know you ought to replace Rebel. I know how much you miss her."

The puppy kept bringing a little ball back to me while I listed every reason we should not even think about taking her home. "Dan would have a fit. He doesn't think he wants another dog. And our lifestyle really isn't right to have a dog. Besides, the church might not like the idea of me housebreaking a puppy with that new carpeting in the parsonage. And then too, who knows what this dog will look like when it is grown? Sure, it's just about the cutest pup who ever lived right now, but still it is a mixture of two breeds. Maybe it'll look dumb as it gets older. And besides, it's too much money."

By now, the little puppy who was just a baby, of

course, was growing tired. I picked her up and she laid her head on my shoulder and tried to snuggle under my neck. I was covered with that delicious smell of puppy breath once again.

Resolutely, I motioned for the sales girl to take her away. "She is sweet, but I'll have to check with my husband," I said as we gathered our things.

"Don't delay too long. I sold her sister yesterday. And two of her brothers found homes this morning. Would you want me to put a HOLD sign on her cage?"

Shaking our heads, we escaped and went to lunch. That evening we told Dan all about the dog. He just smiled and said, "That's nice." I knew the answer was no.

Our daughter came to visit from South Carolina the next day. We hadn't seen her in nearly a year, and we had many things planned. Going to the mall had not been on the agenda, since Dan hates shopping so much that he almost breaks out in hives when he pulls into the parking lot. However, Sonya needed to get a pair of socks (packing for trips is not her strongest skill), so Dan reluctantly headed the car toward the mall.

Well, it just so happens that you have to pass by the pet store to get anywhere in the mall. Since all of us are dog lovers, of course we went in. The saleslady recognized me. "She's still here, waiting for you to take her home!" she stated. Dan and Sonya both proclaimed her to be Rebel's twin, but we were in a rush and had to keep moving.

The next day found us at a larger mall in a neighboring city because Sonya had decided to take a souvenir of her home state back to a friend. Of course, we walked by a pet store in this mall also. This store had full-blooded schnauzer pups that were nearly twice as big as my little schnoodle friend. We held one and smelled its "puppy breath" (my kids have the same weird nose for scents that I have), but there was no spark to this encounter. I didn't think the pup had much personality, but Dan wisely pointed out that if we were going to get a dog, this was the better buy.

"This one is full-blooded with registration papers, and it costs less," he said. I just shook my head. I couldn't have bonded with that pup if I had been paid to do so.

Sonya's visit went all too quickly. It seemed that we were taking her back to the airport only hours after her arrival, though in reality it had been a few days. She had chosen to fly home on Memorial Day, since planes are usually not as crowded and air fare was cheaper then. Goodbyes are never easy for me so I was still drying my eyes and blowing my nose when I noticed that the car did not seem to be heading home.

"Where are we going?" I asked.

"You'll see," responded my smiling husband whose eyes were still a bit red also.

I'm sure you can guess the rest of the story. We arrived at the mall just as they were closing early for the holiday. My saleslady met us at the door and said, "Oh, I am so glad you came back! Another lady looked at the pup, but I told the others here in the store that this puppy and you were just meant for each other. If it weren't for all the dogs I have at home, I would have taken her. She's just about the sweetest little pup we have ever had in the store. She never barks! I want her to go to an extra special home, and I just know she is supposed to be with you." The choice had been made.

The choice was not made in a logical manner (logic has never been my strong suit); it was made from my heart. I was reminded of my favorite poem from an American literature class in high school, entitled "The Road Not Taken" by Robert Frost. I have never been able to remember all of it, but there is something about two roads diverging in the woods. It ends with the phrase "I took the one less traveled by and that has made all the difference." In my husband's sermons he often unknowingly reiterates the principle in the poem by reminding us that "Choices have consequences."

The choice I made that Memorial Day has made all the difference in my life. I chose with my heart, but I have never been sorry because it turned out to be one of the best choices I have ever made.

In Ephesians 1:4, the apostle Paul tells us: "God chose us before the foundation of the world that we should be holy and without blame before Him in love." It was not a logical choice for God to make, but I think He made it out of love. I think He chose with *His* wonderful heart. I hope to live my life in such a way that He will never be sorry.

2

The Christening

The question of what to name this little pup somehow came to be of monumental importance to us, perhaps because we don't have grandchildren we can lavish with love. Or perhaps because there had been a number of other dogs in our lives, and some of them had not lived up to their names. Or perhaps it's because we are just a little "over the edge" when it comes to names. We struggled with this question as if the sun would not come up the next day if we chose the wrong name.

The first dog in my life had been a beagle mix named "Tippy" because of the white tip on her tail. She was our pet from the time I was in fourth grade until the year I got married. She had been a wonderful playmate, but I often felt that we should have given her a more distinctive name, since in the 50s it seemed there was a dog named Tippy on every block. The only name chosen more often for a dog was Spot, and I was sure that was because of the Dick and Jane series of books, which everyone read in elementary school. So I was determined that we should pick a name of distinction for this darling pup. No Tippys or Spots for me!

Early in our marriage we had a poodle named Lucky. The only problem was that Lucky was not a lucky dog; it seemed she was very accident prone. But then, who could blame her, she had to be confused. You see, we had bought her as an Easter gift for our children who were only ages three and one at the time. She had been tiny, almost too small to leave her mother, yet there she was on Easter morning being carried around by a toddler who kept calling her "Bunny." To make things worse, we already had a pet cat at the time whose name was Bimbo (don't ask!). To prevent Lucky from howling and keeping the kids awake, we finally placed Bimbo in the cage with her that first night. On Easter morning I awoke to hear my husband laughing himself sick. Lucky was trying to nurse on the kitten, Bimbo. Poor Lucky probably didn't know whether she was a bunny, a cat, or a dog.

Her worst luck came when she was a little older, perhaps six months or so. One of our favorite pastimes that summer was to go bike riding. Our son rode on the front of his dad's bike, and my bike had a carrier on the back for our daughter. To keep Lucky from feeling left out, we decided to try to train him to ride in the basket on the front of my bike. That was when we discovered Lucky's propensity toward motion sickness. I don't think we ever made it more than a few blocks from home without stopping to clean up the mess in the basket.

After Lucky, there had been a border collie mix named Elsa (after the lion in 'the movie *Born Free*); a fox terrier named Abby (the feminine version of Abraham, since we had purchased her on Lincoln's birthday); and a poodle named Libby.

Miss Libby (short for Liberty, purchased on July 4th) had some real problems. First of all, she was a mix between a standard and a miniature poodle. That alone should not have been a problem. One would think, "A poodle is a poodle." But as Libby grew, it appeared that her back legs were those of a standard poodle while her front legs belonged to a miniature. Her back sloped forward at about a 45° angle. "But looks are not all that matters in a dog," we told ourselves. The problem was that Libby was rather short in the brain department also. My parents had a very intelligent poodle named Buffy at the time. They would bring her along when they came to visit us with the hope that Libby would learn some things from Buffy like, for example, the most elementary game of all for dogs— fetching a toy. No matter how long we would toss the toy and say, "Libby, go get it," she would simply wait for Buffy to chase the toy and then she would chase Buffy, nipping at her legs every step of the way. Buffy would turn to her and bark, "You idiot! Chase the *toy*, not me!" but Libby never understood. The real problem with Libby, though, was that she was untrainable in every department, not just toy chasing. We only had her six months because she never understood where she was supposed to "do her business." Obviously, this was in the days before the advent of the pet psychiatrists (found in every town of any size nowadays), who are eager to help us frustrated owners. So Libby went to live elsewhere.

When our kids were in junior high, we had a sweet schnauzer named Mandy. In fact, Mandy was a name with such good memories that it was in the top five of those we were considering for our little schnoodle, but somehow it seemed almost sacrilegious to name one pet for another that had died. "If I were to die, would you name another kid Kyer?" was a question my son had asked at age five. That question eliminated "Mandy" from the running.

The recently departed Rebel's name had been chosen because of my husband's great love of the Civil War. The other reason we had chosen it is because we both love the Southern states, especially Tennessee. It is our dream to someday live near the Smoky Mountains. Both of our kids live below the Mason-Dixon Line and are even beginning to pick up southern drawls, so we wanted to choose a name that had some sort of southern connotation. "Shiloh" was a consideration, but there is a beagle movie-dog by that name, so it didn't seem to fit.

Dan and I had reached a stalemate. We thought and thought, but could come up with nothing original that seemed to fit our new little friend. Eventually we turned to the rest of the family for their input. When we asked our daughter who lived in South Carolina at the time, she laughed and said, "The answer is so obvious. I can't believe you didn't think of it. If you want to give her a distinctively southern sounding name, what could be better than Dixie? You know, like the song 'I wish I was in Dixie!'"

We looked at each other and simultaneously said, "Duh!" Dixie she became!

Though none of our other pets had ever had two names, Dan said, "Let's call her Dixie Lee!"

Now I was sure he had really lost it. Dan's middle name is Lee. This man who had not even wanted a pet now was willing to share a middle name with the pup. I agreed, but couldn't keep from asking, "You want her to have your name?"

"Not after me!" he responded. "After the greatest general of all time—Robert E. Lee!" Oh, right!

Did you ever think about how funny names are? Even new parents often struggle with what to name their children. We wanted our kids to have distinctive names—no Johns or Susies for us! So we chose Sonya Renee for our firstborn, after a friend of mine. Our son was christened Kyer Toney, after a singer from a gospel quartet we admire. Later we found out that Kyer is a derivative of Hezekiah, the biblical king whose life was lengthened as a result of prayer. Within five minutes of our children's births it would have seemed awful to call them by any other name.

It was the same with Dixie Lee. Once it had been chosen, we could not have called her by any other name.

God also seems to think names are pretty important. In Genesis 17:5 he changed Abram's name to Abraham. Abram meant "high father." Abraham means "father of many nations." Since all Jews, Christians, and Muslims trace their lineage to Abraham, obviously God knew what He was doing.

In the New Testament book of Acts, we find that people who followed the teachings of Jesus were first called "Christians" in the town of Antioch. I heard a sermon by an old time country preacher once in which he explained that the term Christian means Christ's Ones. He went on to say, "If you ain't gonna live like Christ did, then don't call yourself a Christian!" What a challenge!

I remember a time, later in life, when my Dad was feeling rather discouraged because someone he knew had just inherited a large sum of money. You see, Dad had worked hard at a factory his whole life, raising five children on a factory worker's pay. Back then, there was a very distinct difference between the wages of blue collar workers and white collar ones. He mentioned with a heavy sigh that he would never have much inheritance to leave to his children.

"Dad," I said, "don't fret! You have given us something far better than any inheritance."

"What's that?" he asked, with a non-believing look on his face.

"You have given us a wonderful name! Oftentimes when I meet new people I tell them that my maiden name was 'Wood.' Then many of them ask me if my father's name is Floyd. When I say 'Yes,' they go on to tell me what a wonderful man you are and how much they have always looked up to you and respected you. I think the fact that everyone admires our name because of you and Mom is a far better gift than any inheritance we could receive. I feel that there are two names I need to uphold and live up to—Wood and Christian! Both are tall orders."

The hug I got in response to my reply spoke volumes. Dad needed to hear that.

The writer of Proverbs put this whole matter of names in proper perspective when he said: "A good name is rather to be chosen than great riches."

William Shakespeare wrote, "What's in a name? That which we call a rose by any other name would smell as sweet," but I disagree! I believe we need to choose wisely, even if it is just a puppy we are naming. And then I believe it is the responsibility of the one who has received the name to live up to it.

Our little dog's heart is as big as all the land area once called Dixie. And as she grows, she is becoming as brave as the great southern general, Robert E. Lee, and truly lives up to her name.

3

Our First Night Together

That first night, we had done everything the puppy books tell you to do. We played with her for a long time. Dan and I positioned ourselves about 6 feet apart, sitting Indian style on the floor. We rolled the ball back and forth between us, while Dixie chased it again and again. Sometimes she caught it, but then would immediately look confused and run to us with it. Of course this enabled us to keep the game going, but I am not sure she understood much about the rules. After a while, she just gave up and tried valiantly to crawl up into my lap. I eventually picked her up and cuddled her, and she immediately fell asleep.

The books tell you to take the puppy outside for one final potty break before putting them in their bed for the evening. We tried, but she was so exhausted she could not wake up. When I placed her in the grass, she just snuggled down and curled up in a ball.

Enough of this, I thought, and placed her in her cage.

The books had instructed us to make her feel as if she was in a safe place, so we put an old jacket of mine in the bottom of the cage. Since she had been crawling all over me during the evening, we knew the scent would be familiar to her. It also suggested that we place a wind-up clock under the bedding material, since the ticking sometimes reminds the puppy of its mother's heart beating. The book said, "At this point, you have done all you can do to make the puppy happy. Turn out the light, close the door, and go to bed yourself in a room as far removed from the puppy as possible."

It wasn't long before the sleepy, contented, wonderfully warm little bundle of fur who had been so exhausted she couldn't even stand up to potty in the yard was instantly wide awake and howling her little heart out. It was the most pathetic cry I have ever heard.

Dan pulled me away from the door and said, "C'mon. I'm tired. Let's go to bed. She'll quit after awhile."

Of course he was snoring nearly before his head hit the pillow, but my heart kept aching for the our new little baby, all alone in the dark with no one to cuddle her, stroke her fur, and tell her that it would be okay. Some people say dogs do not have a memory. If that is true, why would they care when they are suddenly alone?

I feel certain that Dixie's howls were really words. She was saying:

"Wait a minute! What's happening here? Just a few days ago I was laying close to my Mommy and all my brothers and sisters. I could always reach out and touch someone in my family. Then they took us to that place where we didn't have Mommy any more. I missed cuddling with her and having her lick my fur. We weren't in the nice big, warm brown box at this new place.

"They put us in small metal cages where we could see out in every direction, but we couldn't get out to play with the people who looked at us until some big person opened the door. I still had the rest of my family, though—my sister and I were in one cage and my three brothers were in the cage next to us. We laughed and played with each other. Then they took my sister away, and she never came back. I missed her when I wanted to play so they gave me something to play with that squeaked! I didn't understand the squeak language.

"I wanted my sister back to tug on my ears and tail and yip at me in my language. When I got sleepy, there was no one to cuddle with. When they put a little pillow in my cage, I curled up on it and pretended that it was my sister. I tried to be positive because I still had my brothers right next door. Then two of my brothers were taken out of the cage at the same time, and they never came back. I envied them because it looked like the people who carried them out of that big place were so happy, and they got to stay together. But my brother in the next cage said, "Cheer up, you. We still have each other." That is why it makes me so sad to think that he is still there in that place with all the bright lights and happy smiling faces. He is all alone. And oh, now I am all alone too! I want my family. It's too dark here. I'm scared. Won't somebody help me?"

I cried along with the puppy. I missed my extended family also. One day my dad went away in a box and he never came back either. They say he went to a better place and I know that is true, but I still miss him and wish I could talk to him. I have four older brothers, but people and circumstances came and took them and now they live far away. Like Dixie, I wish I could be with them more. My children grew up and moved away from home. I want to be able to "reach out and touch" my family, but it costs too much to do very often. As I listened to Dixie's pathetic howls, I shed a few tears of empathy, but then I began to thank God for the fact that I have Dan. He is such a wonderful husband, and I can cuddle with him. But that thought made me feel even more sorry for little Dixie.

You can guess what happened. After awhile, I got up and let her out of her cage. Still dressed in my robe, I took her out in the backyard. She was such a smart pup. The minute I stood her in the grass, she did "her business," and when we went inside, she ate a few bites of food. We played with an old sock for awhile until she began to tire out. I picked her up and snuggled her close for several minutes. I told her, "There is nothing to be afraid of, little girl. I am here and I already love you. Now be a good girl, go to bed, and go to sleep."

This time I listened to my heart instead of following what the books said. I lit a small light in her room and turned on a radio station with soothing music, letting it play softly. I sat beside the cage and watched while she nestled in my old jacket and fell asleep. Then I went to bed and both of us slept all night. The next day we moved her cage into our room since I was convinced she was afraid to be alone. She gave us no more bedtime woes. I think she just needed to hear our breathing to relieve her fears. And so I wonder, are puppies really very different from people?

I remember when my husband and I moved into a bad area of town to do rescue mission work. The first day we lived there we watched as several police cars screamed up to the house directly across the street. The officers jumped out and leveled high powered rifles at every possible escape route. Soon they entered the back of the residence and brought three men out the front door in handcuffs. I noticed they were carrying a large plastic bag filled with a white powdery substance. It was like watching a crime show on TV, but it was practically in our laps. That night when we went to bed, I admit that I was frightened. If it had been possible, I might have howled like Dixie, but I think God came to my "cage" and picked me up and cuddled me. He reminded me of a Bible verse in

Hebrews 13:6—"So we may boldly say: 'The Lord is my helper; I will not fear. What can man do to me?'" A great peace enveloped me as I felt that God was there to protect me.

Another incident also came to my mind that first night with Dixie—an incident that we laugh about to this day. Our children were both raised in a city. When our son was 17, my husband took a youth pastorate on the very edge of town. By the evening of the first day, the house was still in a bit of disarray with unpacked cartons scattered about, but we had done just about all we could do. The kids had worked hard so I suggested that we all give ourselves permission to go to bed. Kyer had only been in bed a few minutes when he bounded down the stairs of the new house, wide-eyed and white as a ghost. "I heard a weird noise. It came from that direction. It sounds spooky."

Dan and Kyer went outside arming themselves with flashlights. Evidently Sonya had fallen asleep instantly for, despite the commotion, she did not appear at the stairway. I stood in the un-curtained living room, feeling vulnerable and wondering what they would find outside. Soon they came back in, laughing uncontrollably. Dan punched Kyer in the arm playfully, and he went up the stairs with a red face. It turned out what Kyer had been afraid of was the mooing of cows in the barnyard across the road!

Watching Dixie "face her fears" that first night she lived with us reminded me that some fears are real and some are just sleepy cows, but all can be given to God, who promises in Hebrews 13:5 never to leave us or forsake us.

4

Conquering Fears

For the first several days we had Dixie, I carried her up and down the five steps to our back deck. The steps are open wooden slats, and I was afraid she would fall through the openings and land head first on the concrete patio below. Having already had a pet with impaired brain power many years ago (the aforementioned Libby), I was determined that Dixie would not be brain damaged as a result of a fall. Now it seemed like it was hundreds of times each day that I had to stop whatever else I was doing to grab Dixie and make a run for the back door, down the steps, and into the fenced yard where I would walk around with her and praise her when she accidentally squatted.

I repeated over and over, "Big girl! Yes, her is just

a big girl! Such a smart big girl, too!" (Why is it, I wonder, that normally mature, well-spoken individuals turn into baby-talking fools at the sight of a puppy?) Then I would walk back to the steps, pick her up, and carry her back into the house.

This went on for about a week until my husband said, "Some day you are going to have to let that dog walk down the steps by herself, you know. She will never truly be housebroken until she can do it all by herself."

I glared at him. "She is too little. She might fall. Besides, haven't you ever read the poem called Footprints in the Sand?"

He laughed. "Don't tell me you are going to spiritualize housebreaking a puppy. Of course I've read the poem, but how does it apply here?"

"It says that a man had a dream in which he walked along the beach with the Lord. Across the sky flashed scenes from his life. During each scene there were two sets of footprints, his and the Lord's. But then he noticed—"

"I told you I know the poem," Dan interrupted. "At the times that were hardest for him, there is only one set of footprints. He asks the Lord why He left him at the hardest times, but the Lord replies something like 'That is when I was carrying you.' I still don't see how this all applies to housebreaking the dog."

I was sure that the steps were too high, and she might fall and hurt herself. This was a hard time in the life of this little puppy. How could Dan not see the connection between my carrying Dixie at this hard time to when God carries us at a hard time? The look I gave him said all that and more!

He just shrugged. "She's your dog," he muttered. "And if you always want to have to carry her outside, it's your business."

A few days later, it poured rain all day. I grabbed the umbrella and made a mad dash to the yard each time Dixie indicated a need to go outside, which was approximately every 15 minutes. And when I would put her down in the grass, she either huddled at my feet, whining "Pick me up!" or dashed around the yard in huge circles like a crazed laboratory mouse finally set free, splashing and getting herself all muddy. I was suddenly no longer comparing myself to a caring Lord who was carrying His frightened child! I told myself how silly it was—the puppy had to learn to maneuver the steps sooner or later. The next warm, sunny day would be set aside to teach her how.

Dixie learned to go up the steps on the deck before she learned to go down them. This amazed me, since I compared the physical process involved from a human standpoint. She sat at the bottom and tenaciously pulled herself up onto something approximately twice her own height. Since I am about five feet tall, I tried to imagine reaching up and pulling myself up onto something ten feet tall. Impossible! And yet, she slowly learned to do it. After that monumental effort, she had to do it again and again. Five times! It amazed me that she kept on trying until she succeeded. I stood on the deck and kept calling her name, telling her with each step how she was the bravest little puppy in the world. Evidently, when she was looking up she was not nearly as frightened as when she was looking down.

It struck me how her reactions are so like mine. When I face a big obstacle, I do so much better if I look up than if I look down.

Then came the harder part to teach her—going down.

"C'mon, Dixie. You can do this. Her is such a big girl. Her can maneuver the mean old steps. C'mon down."

She sat atop the deck, stared at me, and whined. "I'll fall. It's too far. Please pick me up," she seemed to say.

I continued to plead and cajole. I reminded myself of Johnny, the announcer on *The Price Is Right,* when I shouted, "Dixie Lee, c'mon down!"

She continued to tell me by her sad eyes, wagging nub of a tail, and whines that it was too high. "I'll fall!" she seemed to say. So I stood right beside the steps and literally took her paws, placed them down on the next lower step, and nudged her bottom until she went down each step, one at a time. It was heart-rending to watch because she seemed so frightened. I kept reassuring her that I would not allow her to fall, but she had not been with me long enough to have memories of my protecting her.

Unlike her, when I am at a hard place in my life, I *do* have a history to remember. In that history, God has never let me fall. In a sermon he gave one day, my husband said that remembering God's faithfulness in our past should cause us never to fear the future. He has never failed us in the past, so why should we think He will not help us with the problems we face today or tomorrow?

Later when Dixie was a few months old, we laughed as she ran up and down the steps. Now she never even thinks about what a huge obstacle she once had to overcome. Like the sports shoe commercial says, she just does it.

By the way, she was also completely housebroken within just a few weeks of her coming to live with us. To this day, however, there is an idiosyncrasy to her personality that could be embarrassing to Dan. Because of the way I bragged on her sometimes to get her to do her business, we have to tell her to "Go be a big girl!" Almost always, the minute she hears those magic words she will run down the steps, potty, and come back up the steps smiling. I think my husband is glad at those times that we live way out in the middle of nowhere. If we were in town with close neighbors, I suppose it would embarrass him to have to tell his dog to "be a big girl."

Regarding the poem "Footprints in the Sand"— someone has written another stanza to the poem. In this stanza the man having the dream noticed that the trail of prints was usually straight and regular, but at various times there would be strange, erratic patterns. When he asked the Lord why there was such a differ- ence, the Lord replied, "My child, don't you under- stand? Those prints were made when we danced!"

Now that Dixie has conquered her fear of the

steps, there are many times when she wants to be outside for the sheer joy of it all! She runs in huge concentric circles, changing directions periodically. This past winter when the snow was on the ground, her footprints looked strangely erratic. Some would be very far apart as she bounded in her crazy dance steps.

Dixie Lee has definitely lived up to her middle name and conquered her fear of the steps as bravely as Robert E. Lee rode his great white horse, Traveller, into battle. Last summer, she actually jumped from the top step to the ground. But, you see, she wanted to dance!

How many times do we let fear keep us from enjoying life? Why can't we learn that God will not let us fall? Many times we need to look up instead of down. When will we learn to overcome our fears in order to enjoy "dancing" with our Lord?

When Dan was in Vietnam during the late 60s and early 70s battling for the right of the Vietnamese people to be free, there were many times when I was overcome by fear. Looking back on those days, I remember that it was when I looked down at the television and listened to Walter Cronkite that I was afraid. When I looked up at God and remembered His promise to be with us, the fear dissipated and I could face the future. I used to walk all over the house singing, "Because He lives, I can face tomorrow."

As I am writing this book, our country is again at war, trying to free the people of Iraq. These are again uncertain days. One of the young moms in our church called me and asked how she can help her small children face the future. I was taken back to those uncertain days early in our marriage and told her to turn off the television and teach the kids to look up, not down. "Sing songs to them about God's protection. Dance around the house with them in your arms and remind them that God is in control." Even as I said it, I wondered if God wants us to dance every day in the security only He can give.

One day Dixie jumped off the couch and landed at an odd angle. She yelped in pain and then proceeded to hold up one of her front paws. She tried to put it down, but whined and immediately drew it back up. This went on for several hours. I took her out back to play, thinking that if it was not truly hurt she would forget about it and begin using it again. But, alas! She looked like the proverbial "arithmetic dog"—putting down three and carrying one.

Obviously, she conquered her fear of heights a bit too well. This time she had jumped too far, and I feared she had broken her leg. So we carried her to the car and drove 15 miles to the Vet clinic, arriving almost at closing time. As she walked into the clinic, she limped pathetically. However, the minute she got inside, a strangely miraculous transformation took place. You see, the lobby was full of big dogs and she was petrified. She ran in little circles at our feet, using *all four* of her paws. She jumped up on my lap, landing on the previously disabled paw without the first sign of pain.

Dan and I just looked at each other in dismay. Then we began to laugh. Could it be that Dixie had developed the fine art form of acting along with all of her other talents? It certainly seemed so. Dan said that he would take her outside to do her business while we waited to see the Vet. I watched out the window, and the dog walked on all four feet with no problems whatsoever. It appeared that her fear of the big dogs had taken away her imagined injury, so we brought her back home without seeing the Vet that day.

How like us this little dog is! Her fear of heights was conquered the day that I stood with her and repeatedly told her that I would not allow her to fall. Now sometimes she jumps from places she should not, thereby momentarily hurting a paw. We still do not allow her to fall, but sometimes she jumps.

At times I get so sure of myself that I try to do things in my own strength which I never should. Those are the times that I believe our wise heavenly Father allows me to hurt myself a bit, so that the next time I will remember to rely on Him.

Sometimes I worry about how I have been hurt. I am not faking it, for I really do get hurt sometimes. But then, in His wisdom, God allows something bigger to come along. It is then that I say, "I can't believe I was worrying about that little mishap. It is nothing compared to this."

For example, I remember fussing about a time when I thought a woman in our church had purposely refused to speak to me. Like Dixie, I was "carrying my paw" and waiting on her to apologize to me. Then we got word that her mother had been diagnosed with breast cancer that week. The next time I saw her, I forgot about my imagined injured ego and put my arms around her. I was walking on all fours again because she was battling a very big dog.

Sometimes it is all a matter of perspective.

5

A Place of Refuge

The puppy books all endorse using a cage or a
specially designed box to help train your new
friend. The theory is that a fairly intelligent
pup will learn very quickly not to make a mess in its
own bed. The book told us to put a divider in the pen
so that one area is for sleeping and the other area is for
"other things." I did not want Dixie to do "other
things" in her cage. I wanted her to do that outside in
the yard, so we did not divide the pen. We just made it
a friendly, warm bed for her.

The book also reminded us that puppies are just
like newborn babies and need to sleep more than half
of every 24 hour period. So, after a time of heavy-duty
playing, when Dixie began to yawn we would carry her
to her bed. She soon learned that the cage was not a

bad place. It came to be her place of refuge. The cage also allowed us to go away for several hours at a time without being concerned that the new puppy would find an inappropriate toy to play with while we were gone. (Early on in our marriage, we had been gone when a pup chewed all the way through electrical wires to our stereo.)

Pastors need to visit their parishioners quite a bit, for example, when someone is admitted to the hospital or other family emergencies arise. Since our congregation seemed to deeply appreciate the times when I was able to accompany Dan on these calls, I decided to train Dixie to willingly go to her cage whenever necessary so she would be safe while we were gone. Milkbone puppy treats were the bribe.

Whenever we needed to leave, I ran toward Dixie's cage, calling her name. Upon her approach to the cage, I bragged on her and tossed a treat into the cage. As soon as she entered the cage to get the treat, I shut the door. Sometimes she gives me a "You tricked me!" look, but the treat always seems to take away the sting of the offense.

Now that Dixie is an adult dog, people are amazed to watch this scenario. Dixie can always sense when we are leaving and usually follows at my heels through the house, wondering if this is a time when she will get to accompany us. But when I open the pantry door and reach for the Milkbone box, she charges back down the hallway and waits for me inside her cage. I tell visitors to stand in the hallway and watch what happens. Invariably they ask, "How did you train her to do that?" It was simple, I suppose. Someone named Pavlov proved a long time ago that a dog would respond to the ringing of a bell. Is it any wonder, then, that Dixie would respond to the sound of a Milkbone shaking in the box? Probably not.

I like to think that Dixie truly enjoys being in her cage. To her it is a place of refuge. She proves that this is true when we periodically find her asleep in her cage with the door wide open. It is not a place where she is forced to go. She chooses of her own free will to enter it because it's her safe, warm place.

Oftentimes we have meetings of different church boards and committees in our living room. When she was a puppy and we weren't sure how she would respond to different situations, we always placed Dixie in her cage during these meetings. The people involved acted as though they thought it was terrible punishment, but we never heard Dixie complain. She munched her Milkbone treat and then settled down, quietly awaiting the time when the strangers were gone and she could romp and play with us again.

I think people need a place of refuge as much as a newborn puppy does. We need to have a place that feels safe and quiet and warm in our lives, a place where we can "hide" from the strangers, re-charge our batteries, and prepare to go back out into the world and face whatever life throws our way.

For me, my place of refuge is anywhere that I can find to spend a few minutes alone with God. I try to talk to Him in prayer about my day. Then I open the Bible and read a little bit, asking God to speak to me through His written Word. God is always willing to meet me at these times, and if I am quiet and listen long enough, He talks to me.

Unlike Dixie, I do not have a cage. Therefore my place of refuge changes from time to time. When my children were small, it was often the bathroom! (What mother has not experienced the times when a bathroom is the only place she can get completely away from family responsibilities!) But even that did not always work. I can remember the times when I would be in the bathroom and see a little finger wiggling at me under the door and hear a little voice saying, "Mommy, when are you coming out? I miss you."

Even in those busy days I think we need to remember that we need to make time for ourselves and for God. Someone has penned a beautiful worship song in which God is supposed to be speaking to someone on this subject. In that song God says, "I miss My time with you." If, as the Bible tells us in Mark 1:35, even Jesus found it necessary to get away from it all to spend time with His heavenly Father, what makes us think we don't need to do the same?

Our children are less than two years apart. Therefore when Kyer began to crawl, Sonya was just a toddler. Oh the scrapes they could get into! Sonya had a family of dolls in her room that she mothered every morning. When I was busy feeding Kyer or bathing him, I would often find that she was doing the same with her dolls. They were very real to her. Is it any wonder, then, that she exploded in motherly rage when she found her baby brother chewing on the foot of one of her "children"?

It became apparent that each of our children needed a place of refuge to spend some time apart from each other. Or, better stated, I needed them to each have a place of refuge to maintain my sanity. So the old playpen came out of the storage shed and reclaimed its place in the corner of the living room. It was then that we began to watch a strange phenomenon take place.

In the beginning, it would be Sonya who would come to me and say in her very grown-up two-and-a-half-year-old voice, "Will you put Kyer in his playpen. He is getting into my things!" But in a few days, Kyer began to crawl to his playpen, pull himself up using the mesh sides, and pound on it. If I was busy and didn't see him do this, there would soon be a wail accompanying the pounding. As soon as I put him into his "cage," he was satisfied.

This continued to happen much longer than any baby rearing book (most of which thought playpens in general would thwart a child's growth) allowed for it. We have pictures of Kyer happily playing in his playpen long after he could walk. You see, it was his place of refuge. He had a super highway system of little cars in there with him, and we heard him giggling as he crashed them into one another. Sonya was happily caring for her babies on the other side of the room with no interference from her brother. All was right with the world.

Was I a terrible parent to separate my children this way? I don't think so. They each needed a place of their own. Indeed, after Kyer outgrew the playpen, we still used a gate across the doorway into Sonya's room. It was much easier to lift her across the gate or step over that gate ourselves than it was to constantly tell Kyer, "Stay out of your sister's room." Of course there were times when they played happily together. But I believe that is because they each knew that they had times when they did not have to be together. Some toys were distinctively his, while some belonged to her. We urged them to share, but they were not always forced to give in to the other's wants. Now that they are adults, our children are very close friends. I like to believe that part of that friendship developed because, as children, they were allowed to be individuals.

Our children are grown and have all the freedom in the world. They both tell us that they sometimes cherish solitude. Unlike most of their generation, they often choose complete quiet so they can read.

The world in general does not cherish solitude. Many people do not have a place of refuge, nor would they know what to do with it if they had one. The world in general is a noise-filled place. Many people do not like quiet. In the rare moments when they find themselves in a truly quiet place, many immediately turn on TV, radio, or CD to chase away the peace and quiet.

One of the favorite places Dan and I choose to vacation is a retreat center in the mountains. There are no phones, no televisions, no radios—it is a place of utter stillness. But after the initial shock of being there wears off, we realize that the stillness is broken by the rushing sound of a mountain stream, the scatter of leaves caused by squirrels, and the seemingly infinite number of different bird songs. We refer to these sounds as God's noise. His noise is so much gentler than the noise offered by the world. In the cacophony of this age, God's noise brings peace to our souls.

Now that Dixie is an "adult" dog, of course she has much more freedom than she had as a puppy. However, the cage is still in our bedroom, and she still chooses to go into it and sleeps there every night. She still likes peace and solitude sometimes.

So I can understand why it no longer takes a Milkbone to lure Dixie into her place of refuge. She is a "better dog" when she emerges, whether it is hours or minutes later. With the Psalmist of old, I find that I am a better person when I say with him:

> *God is our refuge and strength, A very present help in trouble....Be still, and know that I am God* (Psalms 46:1,10).

The tenth verse, as translated in *The Message,* particularly speaks to my heart when it says, "Step out of the traffic! Take a long, loving look at me, your High God."

One of the myriad reasons I am thankful that we have Dixie is that when she willingly goes to her cage, I am again reminded that I need to willingly go meet the Lord in my place of refuge.

6

Dixie's Bear

When we brought Dixie home, the book said that we should surround her with things she could play with and chew to keep her from wanting to do it with things she should not. She came home from the store with a squeaky little alligator toy, a rope tied in knots on both ends, a rawhide chew stick, and a ball—four good-sized toys for a very small puppy. We augmented her toy supply by tying one of my husband's white socks into a knot and giving that to her. However, one need immediately became apparent.

You see, I collect teddy bears. At last count, I have about 50 of the plush little friends sitting all around our house, as well as countless figurines of teddy bears. There is one plush bear atop each bed. Some sit in chairs, one protects the stereo speakers atop our entertainment center, and there are many curling up in baskets or scattered on the floor. Our house is a happy place for all the toddlers in our congregation to visit because they know that they can play with "Aunt Raelene's" bears.

However, it must have been a very confusing place for little Dixie. These little animals sitting everywhere looked like they could be her friends. Yet every time she approached one of them, she heard a quick, "No Dixie. Those are not for you." It soon became apparent that something had to be done. So I chose the least favorite of all my bears (a rather plain Jane among bear people) and gave it to Dixie as a gift. Then, whenever she approached one of my bears rather than just telling her "No!" we redirected her attention to her bear.

People told us, "It will never work. You cannot expect a puppy to differentiate between a bear you have given to her and all the other bears still laying nearby." People were wrong. Within just a few days, Dixie understood that one bear was hers to cuddle, chew, and do with whatever she wanted. All the other bears remained off limits.

Dixie's bear became her constant companion. No matter what other toy she was playing with, she would keep her bear alongside of it. There were many times when she was chewing on her sock or the rope but had one paw on the bear. She followed me from room to room to keep abreast of whatever I was doing, but she would never be in a different room from her bear for long. Suddenly, she would dart like a bullet all through the house until she found her bear and then return to her post, bear in tow. It became a security blanket for her.

It was, without a doubt, her favorite toy. When she wanted to play, it was always her bear that she brought to us. After a brief tug of war, we would toss it down the hallway and Dixie would chase it. In those early days, the bear was bigger than Dixie, and it was hilarious to watch her dragging it all over the house. The day inevitably came when one too many tug-of-war games with the bear took its toll. Dixie's bear needed surgery.

When I picked up the bear to assess the damage, you would have thought I had taken Dixie's child away from her. She pranced back and forth and whined. I kept telling her that I needed to make the bear feel better, but she did not understand. All she could see was that I had taken her bear away from her. When I picked up the needle and thread and began to stitch the torn spots on the bear, you would have thought she was an expectant father awaiting the arrival of his first child. She walked back and forth, back and forth, never taking her eye off what I was doing. When the surgery was complete and I tossed the bear back to her nervous owner, the dog immediately lay down and licked the spot I had sewn to try to take the hurt away.

Dixie is now two years old, and she is playing with her fourth bear. The others gave eyes, noses, and even arms to the cause of keeping Dixie happy. They have not all been identical bears, but as soon as one gets to the point where my surgery will not help it, we put it in the garbage while Dixie is asleep and replace it with a new bear. She sometimes sniffs the new bear for a few minutes before beginning to "bond" with it., but she never has to be told that it is her bear. If it is with her stuff, she assumes it is her new friend.

When Dan and I go on vacation, we board Dixie at Dillon's Kennels. While some dogs balk at the parking lot and put on the brakes, Dixie trots in happily and seems to actually enjoy the change of pace the kennel affords. There are probably 30 dog runs all in a row, each with a doggie door that allows the dogs to run outside at will. The ladies who work there all know Dixie and seem to love her. Therefore, they also know all about Dixie's bear, since it accompanies her everywhere she goes. Mrs. Dillon tells us that of all the hundreds of dogs they have who stay with them, Dixie is the only one who has a toy that goes out the dog door with her every time she goes outside and is always carried back inside with her.

One time when we went to pick Dixie up, we all were so happy to see each other that we did not check the bag full of stuff which the kennel lady brought to us. We were getting in the car when she came running out the door shouting, "Wait! I forgot to give you Dixie's bear!" We were thankful the discovery was made before we drove home, because it certainly would have meant a quick return trip.

The last time we boarded Dixie, a very apologetic Mrs. Dillon met us upon our return. "There was a tragedy," she began.

My heart was in my throat, but then I noticed that she was smiling, so I relaxed.

"Dixie's bear met with an untimely death," she said. "Somehow one arm got through the bottom of the fencing between her and the next dog. Well, before we could get to them a great tug of war ensued and the other dog won. Unfortunately, the bear was ripped in half in the process." She brought the bear out of the bag as proof. I had never seen a more dead teddy bear. She went on to tell us that she was thankful the accident had just happened the last morning of Dixie's kennel stay, for she wondered what she would have done without her buddy overnight.

Upon arrival at home, Dixie walked all through the house looking for her bear. I quickly chose a different bear for her and made a ceremony out of the presentation. "Look Dixie! A brand new bear for you!" She instantly took the bear on a run throughout the house to show it their domain, I suppose. As she ran, we deposited her old bear in the trash bag. We are thankful that she is not a prejudiced dog—she has accepted a dark brown bear, a black and white panda, an all black bear, and now this light tan one. Color, size, or shape do not seem to matter to Dixie, as long as she has one bear among the many that is hers and hers alone.

The question begs to be asked. "How does she know which bear is hers?" I have no idea. Some would say it is established by scent. But when we first give one to her, she has not yet had a chance to put her special scent upon it. Some would say it is by sight. But, if veterinarians are correct and dogs are color blind, how can she differentiate her bear from all the others? The only answer that makes sense to me is that we tell her which one is hers and she believes us.

Last Christmas, a very strange thing happened. When we put up our tree, we decided to place an arrangement of bears underneath it on the floor to make it look as though Santa had delivered a whole bagful of bears to the house. Dixie sat back and watched as we decorated the house and put a number of bears from throughout the house under the tree. She never even went near the tree, for we had told her it was off limits, and of course, her bear was not included in the new arrangement on the floor.

On the third Sunday of Advent, one of our parishioners brought me a little gift bag. She said she had been shopping for her grandchildren when she heard a little voice saying, "Can I go live with your pastor's wife?" A darling little teddy bear jumped into her cart, and she brought it to me as an early Christmas gift. When we arrived home, I put the bear with the others under the tree.

While we were eating our Sunday dinner, we noticed that Dixie was not in her usual spot at the edge of our dining room. "Where's the dog?" Dan asked.

We quietly peeked into the living room to see Dixie contentedly playing with the new bear. She was promptly and properly scolded, and given her own teddy bear instead. We thought that would be the end of it.

However, many times over the next few days when our back was turned, Dixie would pick that new little bear from among the many under the tree and begin to play with it. Dan thought he would trick her and put it in the rear of the group, so that she would be forced to go around the others to get to it. Within an hour or so, however, we saw her trotting down the hall with the new bear in her mouth. She was convinced that we had given that bear to her, when nothing could have been further from the truth.

Eventually, I picked up the new bear, now a little soggy and with its hat in disarray. "She just doesn't seem to understand," I said, as I placed the bear on a bench in the study. This bench is about 18 inches high, 42 inches long, and 13 inches deep. It holds three rows of bears, 20 in all. I placed the new little bear in the second row and wedged it tightly between two larger ones while Dixie was outside. *This will solve the problem,* I assured myself.

Imagine my surprise the next day when Dixie was tossing the same new little bear in the air! I thought I was seeing things and went to the study to check. None of the other bears had been moved. There was just the tiny blank spot on the bench where I had placed the new bear. By now it had become a war of the wills, and I was determined to win.

She ran past me joyfully playing with what she perceived to be her new bear.

"Dixie! Drop it!" I demanded.

She ran into the bedroom. I followed. She ran through the bathroom that connects with the guest room. I followed. And then, the phone rang. As I went to answer it, I noticed that she went back into the study. How I wish there had been a camcorder running in the study! After I hung up the phone, I went in search of the dog and found her asleep in the living room with her head on her old bear. When I went into the study, the new little bear had been redeposited in its assigned place among the others on the bench. Though it must have been a tight squeeze, none of the other bears were askew.

After this whole scene repeated itself a few times, we saw that the temptation was just too much for her. We decided to put the new bear among others in a basket that hangs high on a wall. Unfortunately, Dixie saw me move it. It has now been three months since this whole fiasco took place. To this day, Dixie sometimes stands at the wall and stares longingly up at the little bear in the basket.

Why did she decide that this one little bear, which looks very different in size, shape, and clothing from all her other bears, belonged to her? It is a mystery to which we will never know the answer, I am sure.

As I watch the phenomenon of Dixie and the bears, I am reminded of the very first story in the Bible. After God had created everything, He told Adam and Eve that they could eat of every fruit in the garden, except the ones which hung on the tree in the middle of the garden. In the early days, I believe Adam and Eve were content as they ate all the delicious fruits and walked and talked with God in the garden, somewhat like Dixie is with her bear. But then the devil (in the form of a serpent) tempted Eve with the forbidden fruit. Who knows why she could not resist the temptation? Like Dixie with the little Christmas bear, it seemed to call her name and she gave in to the temptation.

I am thankful that there is a verse in the Bible in First Corinthians 10:13 telling us that God always makes a way for us to escape temptation. Sometimes He has to put the little bear out of our reach. Dixie is a happier dog since we did that, for she avoids constant punishment. Even though she sometimes looks longingly at the forbidden bear, I think she knows it was placed where it is now for her own good. Oh, that we could be as smart as this little dog!

7

Walking Nice

The week before we purchased Dixie, one of my favorite programs was on television—the Westminster Dog Show. I love to watch the dogs of all sizes and shapes as they trot around the ring in front of the judges. It is interesting to watch the different trainers and to learn from the way they handle their dogs. In the competition, the top dogs in each breed are judged until a winner is found for each one. Then the dogs that have won the best in their particular category are all put into the show ring together. The crowning moment comes when one animal is judged "Best in Show." I look forward to seeing who will win with almost the same intensity that my husband displays when watching football or baseball. Since I am a good sport and allow my husband first rights on the TV remote most of the time, he indulges me once a year and allows me to watch this event.

As I watched the show just before we got Dixie, I told myself that if we ever did get another dog, we would teach it to walk as nicely on a leash as the dogs in the Westminster show did. You see, with all of the pets we had before Dixie, none of them had ever mastered "Leash Walking 101." Most of them practically pulled your arm out of the socket as they tugged to get as far ahead as possible. It had never been fun to take any of them for a walk.

Rebel, Dixie's predecessor, had come close to mastering the course. In fact, when she was a puppy I actually enrolled her in Dog Obedience School during a hard time in my life. Our son was going through a divorce, and my husband was away from home at a 3 month long Army schooling. I thought it would be a fun diversion from the usual routine, so I signed Rebel up for this class. Imagine our surprise when we arrived to find that she was the only small dog there. Dogs and owners were told to stand in a circle. I carried her to the circle, since all the other dogs were full-grown German shepherds, rottweilers, doberman pinschers, and the like.

The "teacher" (a.k.a. Ms. Hitler) immediately sneered, "Mrs. Phillips, put your dog down!"

The dog next to us was a brindle colored boxer approximately ten times larger than Rebel. Mr. Boxer seemed to have an inordinate amount of interest in Rebel's backside. As a tiny puppy, Rebel had mastered the art of sitting up to beg. She was so frightened of all the big dogs, especially the boxer, that she sat up at my feet in the sawdust circle and begged to be held.

Ms. Hitler never even smiled as she yelled, "Rebel Phillips, there will be no begging in my obedience class!"

On the way home from class that night, I began to cry. It seemed I had no control over my own life just then. Our son's life was in a real mess, and I couldn't even talk to my husband about it, since he was at Fort Jackson in South Carolina and I was in Ohio. And now it appeared that Rebel might flunk obedience school!

Rebel noticed my distress and leaned over to lick the tears off my face. She whined, "Mom, I don't like this obedience school. That teacher is mean. And that boxer was touching me in inappropriate ways."

In one brief moment we made our decision—Rebel was now an obedience school dropout! I decided not to put either one of us through the stress of returning to that class. But I knew that I had never had any talent for teaching a pet to walk on a leash (my main objective in enrolling Rebel in obedience school course). Instead of worrying about it, I just purchased one of the leashes that has a reeling in device that allows the dog the freedom to roam up to 20 feet ahead of its owner. When necessary, the owner can shorten the leash and pull the dog back to her side. As you can imagine, Rebel was usually 20 feet ahead of us on our walks.

I was determined it would be different when we got Dixie. When she was only 8 weeks old, I began to try to train her to walk like the Westminster dogs do—immediately beside and just one step ahead of me.

Have you ever watched a puppy the first time its collar is attached to a leash? Why is it that a normally docile pet becomes a bucking bronco? Why, I wonder, do they hate it so much?

We tried over and over: in the house, in the yard, and along our country road. Sometimes I was dragging her. Sometimes she got a running start and then almost hung herself when she came to the end of the leash. My husband kept telling me that she was too young to learn this task, but I was determined.

I kept my voice calm and repeated a million times, "Walk nice, Dixie." Now I know that is improper grammar, since the adverb form of nice would be nicely, but somehow I doubted whether Dixie cared much about proper grammar. What she mostly cared about in those days was getting herself unhooked from the dreaded leash.

I consulted the puppy training book. It said to get the puppy accustomed to a leash, one should hook the leash to the collar and allow her to walk around in the house with it attached. I tried this, but she got herself tangled around a table leg or the leash became caught on something within just a few minutes each time. I eventually decided that perhaps the writer of the book did know a little about this issue, for Dixie seemed to battle the leash a little less with each lesson.

Within weeks, she knew and understood what it meant to "Walk nice." I hold the handle of the leash in my left hand and then hold the lead going to her collar in my right hand. Dixie walks just beside and a little in front of my right foot. She could be in a Westminster Show and no one would fault her for not walking correctly, most of the time!

Sometimes though, it seems that she just gets ornery. She tugs and pulls on the leash just as ferociously as did all her predecessors. At those times, I can remind her to "Walk nice" till I am blue in the face. Eventually she will calm down, but I fear it is only when she gets tired of the tug and decides on her own to obey.

The walk along our country road takes us past a farm where two big black Labrador retrievers have the free run of the property. Invariably, they come to the edge of the road to growl and snarl at Dixie and me. I have noticed that if Dixie is walking beside me like she should be, she smugly glances at them with a toss of her head that clearly says, "I am with my lady, and she would never let you hurt me!" If, however, it is one of her ornery days when she is far ahead of me, tugging me along, the scene is entirely different. At first sight of the Labradors, she yips and runs to my feet and tries to hide from them. It would appear that she has learned that walking nice has a feeling of safety as one of its rewards.

Each time this scene re-enacts itself I am reminded of a scripture verse found in Isaiah 30:21: "Your ears shall hear a word behind you, saying, 'This is the way, walk in it,' whenever you turn to the right hand or whenever you turn to the left."

I have to admit that sometimes it feels as though God has put me on a leash. And, like a new puppy, I tend to fight the leash for all I am worth. If only I could learn that the "leash" of God is for my own good!

After Dan completed his military service and was honorably discharged, we went back to our hometown where he got a job at a local factory, and we purchased a lovely home just a few blocks from where my parents lived. All was right with my world. My Dad had worked in a factory, and the money he made provided for all of our needs. We had lived a happy life. Now Dan and I would recreate the lives of our parents. Then came the day that, with just one sentence, Dan turned my world upside down!

"Honey, I think God wants me to be a preacher!"

I laughed. "No, He doesn't—'cause He doesn't want me to be a preacher's wife!"

Words flew fast and furious between us. I informed him that I liked the way our lives were right then and did not want anything to change. We went to bed that night with a wall a mile high and equally thick between us. He was miserable. I was miserable. Deep in my heart I knew Dan was right, for God had been directing me toward full time ministry also, but I wasn't willing. I did not want to "walk nice."

I wish I could say that argument only lasted a day, but sadly it went on for weeks. We looked at the idea of ministry from every possible angle. Dan quoted me the verse about delighting ourselves in the Lord and He would give us the desires of our hearts. I stomped my foot and said, "I have the desires of my heart right here, right now. I don't want to change."

Lovingly, the heavenly Father tugged gently at the leash of my heart. Eventually I fell on my knees and sobbed, "Okay. If you want us in a pastorate, I'll go." Our all-knowing God knew that my heart was not in it, but He took me at my word. He knew that I would try to walk nice.

The path has not always been easy—but would I change it if I could? Not one bit. Learning to walk nice with God is a wonderful adventure. If I want to do what God wants me to do, I must stay by His side, remembering that He will tell me which way to go. When Dixie is walking at my side, not ahead or behind, she hears my voice telling her which way we are going to turn and bragging on her obedience. When I am walking close to God, I can hear His voice in my heart telling me which way I should go and bragging on my obedience.

When Dixie is not walking nice and we meet the big dogs, she is immediately frightened and has no sense of peace regarding my protection of her. When I am not walking the way God wants me to and I encounter the "big dogs" in my life, I also lose that sense of peace regarding His protection.

Dixie will never walk into the Westminster ring. As mentioned before, she is a hybrid: a schnoodle. No hybrids are allowed at Westminster. And, of course, she has been spayed, which is another no-no at the dog show. However, when she walks nice (and shh...even when she doesn't!), she is "Best in Show" at the Phillips house.

It is my prayer that I will walk so nice in this life that some day I might receive a crown from my heavenly Father. (But shh...isn't it a comfort to know that He still loves us even when we don't walk nice?)

8

Food and Water

The domesticated animals of the world are the only ones who cannot fend for themselves. All the animals that live in the wild have an inborn sense of knowing how to find what they need to survive: food, water, and shelter. But a pet dog or cat that is suddenly abandoned would die quickly from starvation, dehydration, or exposure. There's nothing much sadder than an abandoned animal. They stumble along the edge of a street or road looking hopefully at every passing car. They must wonder what they did to deserve such treatment in the beginning. But as the hours or days go by I think they are just looking for someone—anyone—who would feed them or give them water.

Dixie Lee was barely weaned when we got her. The

book says that puppies and adult dogs should be reared on dry food with no table scraps. Since I have worked at two different veterinary clinics, this is one issue on which I totally agree with the book. More dogs come into Vet clinics because of something extraordinary they have eaten than for any other reason. So, we purchased a bag of dry puppy chow and took her to her bowl periodically.

Our first problem was that the bowls were too big. She was so tiny she couldn't even see into them. When she valiantly tried to get a drink in the water bowl, she plopped her feet up on the edge of the bowl and spilled it all over the kitchen floor. We resorted to smaller plastic cereal bowls until the next day when we made our way back to the pet store for new bowls and a few other dog accessories.

Dixie turned up her nose on that first evening at the new food. Obviously, her little taste buds were more developed than we had imagined and, like the children of Israel in the book of Exodus, she was longing for the food she had eaten before. We tried hand feeding, cajoling, gently pushing her nose into the smaller bowl—all to no avail.

I was tempted to suggest to Dan that he get down on his hands and knees and eat a bite or two of the food himself, but didn't think that idea would fly with him. I was pretty sure he would bring up how when our children were small I had convinced him that they needed to see Daddy eat cauliflower and liver so they would learn to like it. He had truly gone the extra mile back in those days, burying each bite of liver or the dreaded white vegetable in mashed potatoes and still gagging as it went down. I decided that if he got down on all fours Dixie would either want to play with him or be scared to death, so I didn't mention my idea.

In his resolute way, he murmured, "She'll eat when she gets hungry." Where does he get such wisdom?

She wouldn't eat anything at bedtime. I whined, "But the book says she will go to sleep better if she has a full belly."

He responded curtly, "She has been sound asleep for an hour. Does the book tell you how to wake them up to get them to eat before their little beddy-bye time?"

"There is no need to be so sarcastic!" I retorted, as we walked resolutely toward her cage.

Having already described that first night, I won't go into all the details again. However, the reader will recall that in the middle of the night the puppy did eat. Somehow all the inhibitions about the size of the bowl or the new food disappeared. She ate and drank till her little heart was content.

From that time on, we have never had any problem with her eating habits. After feeding her puppy food for the first year, we switched her to adult chow. She has a wonderful appetite and has never done what the aged veterinarians refer to as "going off her feed."

She does have one quirk in the way she eats that makes us chuckle. Our dining room is beside our kitchen. The dining room is carpeted, while the kitchen has a linoleum floor. Dixie's bowls are at the end of the kitchen, which is farthest away from the entrance into the dining room. Our thoughts in placing them there were simply that they are close to the pantry where we keep the bag of dog food. And then too, should there be any spilling of water or food, it would be on the linoleum and not on the carpet.

However, when Dixie was about six months old, she decided that she preferred to eat on carpeting. And so, every meal takes twice as long for her to eat. She gets a mouthful of food, walks across the 12 foot expanse of linoleum, sits down on the edge of the carpet, drops all the food onto the carpet, and then proceeds to eat it. We have wondered what caused her to ever begin doing this. Is the lighting more to her liking in the dining room? Does she not like to stand on the hard floor? Is it because there are sliding glass doors to the outside where she can have a better "view" as she eats? While the answer could be any of the above, I think she does this strange trot back and forth while she eats for two reasons: 1) in her heart, she believes she is a human, and 2) simply because she can! She knows that she has never seen Dan and I eat in the kitchen. Therefore, since she believes she is just like us, why should she eat in there? But perhaps more importantly, I think every time she does this she thinks she is getting away with something.

You see, the first time she tried this stunt, I told her "No, Dixie!" and picked up every bite of the food and returned it to her bowl. She immediately went to the bowl, got another mouthful of food, returned to the carpet, sat down, and dropped it all over the edge of the rug again. I retrieved it, telling her she was a bad dog and that she was supposed to eat at her bowl. After a couple more replays of this idiotic behavior, Dan intervened on the dog's behalf.

"What will it hurt if she eats on the carpet?" he asked. "As long as she gets every bite, maybe you should just let her. You need to remember that the book says you need to pick your battles."

I couldn't believe he was quoting the book to me. When had he even taken the time to read it? Now I understood why I had found the book in the bathroom several times.

I took his advice and decided to let Dixie win this battle. So, she eats on the carpet. Sometimes I can tell by the jerk of her head that if she could make herself understood she would be sing-songing, "Na na na na na na! I'm eating on the carpet!"

She won that battle, but there is a more important battle regarding food that I won with her. Even though I absolutely love dogs, there is one place that I cannot stand to have a dog. I don't believe they should be anywhere near a table when people are eating. So we have trained Dixie to stay away from the table while we eat. She lies right at the archway between the living room and dining room, no closer than about six feet from the table. Once in a while, she will forget and place herself too close to the action. At those times we just say, "Dixie, where do you belong?" and she will back up. When I say back up, I mean it literally. She stands and looks at us and inches her way backwards toward the magical dividing line between the two rooms, like a race horse backing itself into the stall.

When she gets to "the line," one of us tells her she is a good girl. She smiles contentedly and plops down until we have finished the last bite of our meal. Somehow she understands that the minute either of us stands up, she has freedom to move wherever she wants to again. The only time she gets confused is when I leave the table to serve dessert. At those times, I say, "Not yet, Dixie." She sits back down and waits till we are completely finished before she crosses the line again.

Now that Dixie Lee is a full grown dog, Dan and I have developed a rather bad habit. We each rely on the other one to fill her food and water bowls. And inevitably, there are times when both of us forget. Poor Dixie! At those times she will come and sit directly in front of us and just stare until she gets our attention. Sometimes we are preoccupied with people-type problems. At those times we will say, "Go play, girl. Where is your teddy bear?"

Easily distracted, she will bring her bear for a few romps down the hall. But suddenly, she'll stop and stare again. "Do you want out?" we will ask. And even though she doesn't run to the door, we get up and try to get her to go outside. When she just continues to stare, it finally sinks in—she needs food and/or water.

Talk about feeling like a rat! Apologies abound toward Dixie. Many times I have filled both bowls while saying, "Oh, Dixie—I am so sorry. Why don't you figure out a new way to tell us what you need?" (One of her predecessor dogs carried their bowl and threw it at our feet—obviously, we are slow learners.)

She doesn't snap back like I would. If I were her, I would be saying, "Look! You've had me two years now. I have needed food and water every day of my life. When are you going to learn?" But Dixie just wags her tail and thankfully eats what I put before her. She has never held a grudge in her life. She waits patiently for us to remember to supply her needs and then she accepts what we give her with gratitude.

God has promised that He will give us whatever we need. He instructs us to look at the sparrows and tells us that if He cares for their needs, He will certainly care for ours. If we could only learn to wait with the patience and dignity that Dixie displays, we would be so much better off.

Sometimes I think that I am getting away with something, like Dixie does when she eats on the carpet. Though I would never be so brash as to sing-song a "Na na na na na na!" to God, I may think it in my heart. I may be guilty of "eating on His carpet"— doing something I know He would rather I did not do, almost daring Him to punish me in some way.

There may be times when God tells me not to cross a line, but I teeter on the edge of it. When He says in my heart "Where do you belong?" do I imme-diately back up until He says "Good girl!"?

When God supplies my needs, do I thank Him or do I worry that He will forget to fill my food and water bowls? Perhaps I need to learn the truth of the Bible verse found in Philippians 4:19: "And my God shall supply all your need according to His riches in glory by Christ Jesus."

And after He supplies those things that I need, somehow I should wag my tail to let Him know that I am grateful.

9

Seize the Day!

It is springtime. I go to my closet and pull out an old Army sweatshirt. As I zip the front and begin to pull the hood up, Dixie pads into the room. She is immediately wild with energy, whining and dancing in circles at my feet. I tell her she needs to wait until I get the hood tied, so she sits at my feet trembling from head to toe. I step into the hall and she nearly trips me, running to the refrigerator and back again five times in the length of time it takes me to traverse the hallway. An occasional quiet "yip" escapes her tense little body, and her tail is a total blur as it wags in triple time. Now she is on her hind feet, doing perfect ballet-like movements, backing away from the refrigerator. As I reach atop the refrigerator for her leash, all bedlam explodes. She races to the back door then back to my feet, to the front door then back to my feet. I calmly tell her to "Sit!" With a whine and a nervous little jump step, she tries to obey. Finally, I attach her leash. The reason for all of Dixie's excitement is what she has known since she first spotted the hooded sweatshirt—we are going for a walk!

My doctor tells me that exercise is beneficial. It will lower blood pressure, lower cholesterol, speed up metabolism, and release endorphins into my bloodstream, making me feel better, helping me to sleep better and lose weight, and benefitting me in a host of other ways. Walking, says the doctor, is the easiest form of exercise you can get.

No one has ever told Dixie any of this. Walking, to her, is an adventure! If dogs worship God, perhaps they do it best when they are walking. So while I try to psyche myself into the idea that I need to go for a walk, Dixie prances in anticipation. "Let's go!" she shouts.

To Dixie, it doesn't matter where we go. We can head west on our long country road toward the woods and the little stream, or we can head east to where the road dead ends in a T intersection with a road that has slightly more traffic than ours. On the other hand, we can go immediately across the road and follow the loop that skirts the edge of the cemetery. She is not particular—there will be adventure no matter which path we follow.

Adventure comes in many forms when you are a two year old schnoodle. A pop bottle thrown out of someone's car window looks like a good toy. "Let me smell it. I need to know if it is the kind you drink," she says. A cigarette butt might be a tasty snack. "No, I guess not!" she chokes as she spits it out. I tell her it is dirty and she should leave it alone, but I know tomorrow she will need to taste it again.

"Oh look—a caterpillar!" she shouts. She is immediately in her most playful position—rear end in the air, face down on the pavement, striking gently at the moving bug with her paws. I stop until she loses interest and is ready to move on, which takes approximately 15 seconds.

Now she begins to tug on the leash, not in her walking nice mode at all, for up ahead she has spied some road-kill. "What is it?" she asks as we get closer. "Oh...look! It's the squirrel that has been raiding the bird feeder on the back deck. Why is he laying so still?"

I shorten her leash and tell her that she cannot check this out. "It could have some bugs or a disease that would not be good for you, Dixie," I explain. I am thankful that the road is deserted, and no one can hear me reasoning with my little friend.

If we have headed west, there is the inevitable stop at the bridge where we must check out the water running beneath it. Though we have been across it hundreds of times, and we have never yet seen a fish, you never can tell. Today just might be the day! Besides, sometimes there are little frogs here. "Remember what fun we had chasing one that time last week?" She grins.

This week some wildflowers have bloomed along the edge of the road. Dixie has to smell each one individually. She is just as excited over the first dandelion of the season as she is the crocuses, I notice. Perhaps she knows that God created both of them. I am taken back to the days when my children were small and they brought in a handful of dandelions with different length stems and say, "Mommy, look! We picked you flowers." Those were, perhaps, the loveliest bouquets I have ever received.

Sometimes on our walk there will be a special diversion. If we walk east and turn to the left at the dead end, we can see some cows. Dixie is very brave until we get close to them. Then she stays right beside my feet and growls softly. One time a big cow was laying just on the other side of the fence. From Dixie's perspective, I don't suppose she knew that it was an animal. Perhaps she thought it was just a big black and white rock. She approached it and was on the verge of putting her head through the fence to sniff when the cow decided to stand up and "Moo!" Dixie jumped straight up in the air, and her feet were moving in the air like a cartoon animal. I wished someone was filming us. I laughed hard as I picked her up and consoled her.

If we turn right at the dead end, we come to a farm where an Amish family lives. Their children are almost always outside playing, and often the mom is either hanging clothing on a line in the back yard or working in their huge garden. They all wave hello and Dixie stands up with her front paws on the bottom rail of the fence to greet them. The little boys, with their bare feet and round bowl haircuts, are as happy to see Dixie as she is to see them.

When we turn back towards home, we often enter the cemetery. There are several graves that are on a circuit that Dixie inspects. I have always wondered how she knows which grave belongs to the young man from our congregation who committed suicide during Dan's first year as pastor here. She invariably tugs me toward his grave, and sometimes I sit down on the little bench the family put beside it. I let Dixie roam around a bit as I let my mind wander back.

"Oh Lonnie," I moan. "What were you thinking? How could we not have known how troubled you were?"

I remember watching him from the piano the Sunday before it happened. The congregation was singing a favorite praise chorus: "Shout to the Lord." He was smiling from ear to ear as tears dripped off his face. He even had one hand slightly raised in praise. His beautiful wife and daughter were beside him, and it looked as though everything was perfect in his life.

Then I remember how we had gone on vacation that week. We had one glorious day at the retreat in the mountains when we received the phone call. Our head deacon asked Dan if he was sitting down and explained that Lonnie was "no longer with us." I was standing beside Dan as his face lost all color and he asked, "What do you mean?" Within the hour, we were on our way back home. It was, perhaps, the hardest days we had ever faced in ministry.

As I sit on the bench, Dixie seems to respect my reverie. She lays down at my feet as I bow my head for a few moments. I usually ask God to help us be more perceptive of people's needs. Though all this happened four years ago, I still sometimes shed a tear. Then Dixie will rear up on her hind legs and lick my face and say, "C'mon. We still have things to see."

We walk a bit slower in the cemetery, and I sometimes fix artificial flowers that have blown over. We walk to the far corner and hope to see bluebirds in the special house the local bluebird society placed there. I tell Dixie to be very quiet, and sometimes we are allowed to hear their beautiful song and catch a glimpse of the family.

We usually stop for a moment at the strange grave of little Jerry. It bears a little white marker with a lamb on the top. Cut into the stone is his name and the year 1946. What makes it strange, and of special interest to both Dixie and me, is that every three or four months a brand new teddy bear is placed atop the grave. It is apparent, from the etchings on the stone, that his mother is buried next to him. And so, I wonder, is it an old man who treks to this marker and silently places a teddy bear atop the grave of a baby who has been dead for more than 50 years? I don't allow Dixie to touch the teddy bear. It almost seems sacred. We move on.

As we finish our romp through the cemetery, I check to make sure there are no cars coming on our country road. If all is clear, I sometimes let go of Dixie's leash and say, "Go get Daddy." She fairly flies as she runs to the church steps. She waits patiently at the top step until I arrive to open the door, and then she bounds directly into his office. He usually has the door to his office almost closed, but she pushes it open with her nose and jumps into his lap for a quick kiss on his cheek. Sometimes, if he is not busy, he will ask, "What did the two of you discover on your walk today?"

As I relate to him how Dixie was enchanted with a caterpillar or a butterfly, I realize that Dixie has taught me the invaluable lesson which the author of *Dead Poet's Society* tried so valiantly to relay. *"Carpe Diem!"* the young boys said in Latin. "Seize the day!"

To my little four-legged friend, every diversion from the normal is something to be celebrated. Every tiny leaf or animal can be an adventure. To quote a country love song, she has taught me to "stop and smell the roses." She has taught me that there is adventure no matter where you turn. You just have to look for it.

Sometimes I have my whole day planned out, down to the minute. Then, right in the middle of something really important, I will get a phone call, perhaps from one of the eldest members of our congregation. Sickness and bad weather has kept her house-bound for a few weeks. I look around at the things still on my list of "to do" items and think that I do not have time for this kind of phone call right now. When I spy Dixie in the backyard chasing a leaf in happy, carefree abandon, I sit down and spend a few precious minutes chatting with this dear lonely soul.

Dixie has taught me to seize the day.

Dan is an avid walker for exercise sake alone. He used to run, but as the calendar clicks off the years, he has slowed down a bit. However, he still walks so fast that I can hardly keep up with him. When he is on one of his walking-for-exercise-alone kicks, he does not take Dixie along. She would slow him down too much since she investigates every stone or twig out of place. But sometimes he will say, "Do you want to go for a W?" He thinks if he spelled out the entire word, Dixie would figure it out. But it is too late for that, she runs to the refrigerator in anticipation when he says the W. Together, the three of us walk slowly as we unwind and tell each other all about our day. Dixie seems to be in seventh heaven on these evening strolls. She trots between the two of us, glancing up periodically as if to say, "I love you guys."

We just look at each other, grin, shake our heads, and wonder how we ever got along without her.

10

Indian Giver

Though Dixie seems to us to be so amazingly smart, there is one action we would like her to learn, but which, so far, she is not able to understand. She loves to play with us and will chase toys that we toss down the hallway for hours, taking brief time-outs only to run to the kitchen for a drink of water. However, try as we will, day in and day out, she does not grasp how much more fun this game would be if she would only learn to give us the toy as soon as she retrieves it!

She brings a toy to us and touches it against a leg. At this point, it doesn't seem to matter whether it is the leg of a chair, the couch, or a human being. In the thrill of knowing that a game is about to begin, she loses her peripheral vision and does not distinguish the leg of the player. Many times we have laughed as she pushes her bear, rope, sock, or ball against the table leg or chair leg as if to say, "C'mon—let's play." Eventually, though, she sees the error of her way and touches one of our legs with the toy.

Now, in Dixie's mind the game begins with a tug of war. My husband or I will reach down and try to take the toy away from Dixie so that we can throw it for her to retrieve. We are usually saying, "Drop it, Dixie, so that we can play." But the catch is, Dixie is already playing. A large part of the enjoyment for her seems to be in keeping the toy away from us. So we reach to get the toy, and as she sees a hand coming toward her prized possession, she backs up and shakes the object.

Sometimes we ignore her insistent nudges against our leg, thinking that she will eventually tire of her agenda and then we would pick up the toy and begin playing according to our rules. Those rules would look like this: We throw the toy and Dixie brings it back to us, dropping it at our feet. Simple rules, simple game.

But if Dixie were writing the rules to the game, they would look something like this:

"I take toy to my man or woman and nudge it against their leg. They reach to get the toy as I back up a few feet. (Note: If I am playing with my man, I have to back up farther than if I am playing with my woman, since he seems to be able to reach further than she does.) When a hand is coming toward my toy, I try to keep the hand from retrieving the toy with whatever means available. (Note: This usually will involve rather violent head tossing. A brief growl also helps.)

"Next the human will grab hold of one end of toy. At this point, it is my job to back up and pull hard. (Note: It helps to lower my head and elevate my hind quarters, thus giving me more leverage.) I have to eventually let the human win the tug of war. Not knowing that if they would simply let me have my end of the toy back, we could begin the game all over again, the human will invariably toss the toy as far away as possible. (Note: My man can throw with much more accuracy than my woman can. If she is the one playing, I don't have to run nearly as far because the toy will very likely bounce off the nearby wall.)

"At this point, while I am going to get the toy, the human is likely to repeat some trite phrase repeatedly such as, 'Go get it!' I have tried to tell them by my body language that, of course, I am going to go get the toy, but it is probably best to allow them to repeat the cheer. If they were not doing this, they might understand that after I make this ridiculous trip to get the toy back, we can begin the tugging game again. So rather than allow them to strategize their tugging offense more thoroughly, I pretend that this chasing is what the game is all about. After the trip to retrieve the toy, it is my job to go nudge a leg so that the tug of war game can begin again."

Dixie's actions during this game always makes me think of how I react when God tells me to give something to Him. Like so many other things in life, it is all a matter of perspective. From my perspective, I would rather hold onto whatever it is. I hang on tightly to my home, my possessions, my family (both immediate and extended), and my dreams and goals for the future. When He reaches with His loving hands to take some-thing away from me, I hang on for dear life, fearing that if I give this "toy" to Him, the game will end or He will throw it far away and I will have to run hard to retrieve it. I cannot see that the game would be so much more fun if I would give everything to Him of my own free will and learn to play the game by His rules.

When I was a little girl on Atlantic Avenue in a dis-tant town in northwest Ohio, there were two very popular pastimes for children. All the little girls played "jacks." The object of the game was to toss a ball into the air while picking up little metal objects shaped something like a star and then catch the ball on its way back down. I was never very good at this game. I tried to play it and even had my own little cloth bag (sewn by my mother) in which I toted my jacks back and forth to school. There were some little girls who could go through the game without ever missing the ball on its way back down. You began the game by picking up one jack at a time. In the next round, you picked up two at a time and then three and so forth. You were al-lowed to continue your turn until you either missed the ball or did not pick up the appropriate number of jacks while the ball was in the air. I have often won-dered why I did so poorly at this game. Perhaps my fine motor skills were not well developed, or I was not very coordinated. But I think the most likely reason I was not a good jacks player is that I really did not care to play the game because there was a different one I liked even better.

While all the little prissy girls spread their skirts demurely around them and daintily picked up the jacks, all the little boys were in a large circle in the gravel of the playground playing marbles. While the little girls giggled quietly, the boys cheered, spit, pushed, shoved, and had ever so much more fun. When the bell rang at the end of recess, the little girls retrieved their set of jacks and their little ball, placed them in their bag,and lined up to go inside. The little boys, on the other hand, retrieved all the marbles they had won as well as their original set and put them in their little cloth bag before they got in the line. You see, the girls played their game for sheer enjoyment. while the boys were playing "for keeps."

In marbles, a large circle was drawn by dragging a foot in the gravel. Each boy would dump his marbles (which were nothing more than perfectly round little balls, made of glass) out of his handsewn bag into the center of the circle, spreading them out rather evenly. Each boy held back his favorite "shooter" (which was usually a somewhat larger marble known as a "boulder") and awaited his turn. Then when his turn came, he was allowed to take aim at any and all of the marbles in the circle with his "shooter" and roll it toward the marbles in the center of the circle. All the marbles that he hit were his to keep until the end of the game. Presumably, the boy with the most marbles at the end of the game was pronounced the winner.

Problems arose on the playground when one boy lost his favorite marble to another. Who knows why it was his favorite marble? Perhaps his grandfather had given it to him. Perhaps it was a "purey"—a marble which only had one color. Perhaps it was a "cat-eye"— a clear colored sphere of glass with a colored swirly thing in the middle that made it look like a cat's eye. Or perhaps it was a steely—which was a ball bearing thrown into the glass marble game to give it some extra excitement. Whatever the reason, often there were tears, and the boy who had "lost his marbles" often argued that he had not known the game had been "for keeps."

Unbeknownst to my mother, who I think tried valiantly to turn me into a little lady, I rarely played jacks with the little girls. I was usually in the middle of a bevy of little boys, down on my perpetually skinned up knees, playing marbles for all I was worth. In fact, I usually carried the heaviest bag of marbles in the class because I could shoot so well. I had developed a knack of flicking my thumb against my index finger that sent my shooter barreling into a large group of marbles at top speed. Every marble that moved was quickly put into my bag, and I usually had acquired a few new possessions by the end of each recess.

Thankfully, my teachers were ahead of their time. Many times the boys in the class would whine, "Mrs. Johnson, can't you make Raelene play jacks with the girls?"

Mrs. Johnson would wink at me as she asked, "Why?"

The answer was usually something like, "It's no fair! She has a steely shooter, and she always wins all of our marbles. Sometimes us boys don't want to play 'for keeps,' but she won't give back any marbles she wins."

Like Solomon of old, the teacher turned the question back to them. "Boys, did you agree to play for keeps?"

They would nod their heads sheepishly while saying something like, "But we didn't know she would win all our marbles!"

The teacher intervened on my behalf and said, "She won them fair and square. Maybe you can win them back at recess tomorrow." And the matter would be settled. It is probably a good thing I was a girl who grew up in a time when no little boy would ever hit a little girl, else I would likely have been beaten to a bloody pulp many times over a marble game.

Perhaps, in her own little canine way, Dixie is just trying to play with her toys "for keeps." If only she could realize that if she would give the toy to us, she could learn a new game that is much more fun than an endless game of tug of war.

If only I would realize, in my own little finite way, that when I give everything to God, I find much more peace and fulfillment, and the game of life goes so much more smoothly. That little girl, who didn't like to lose her marbles, doesn't like to let go of possessions or people she loves to see God use them in new and different ways to bring glory to His name.

Those of us who grew up in the 1950s were not politically correct according to today's standards. Anyone who said they were playing marbles for keeps and then demanded, amidst tears, that they be given back their marbles at the end of the game was called an Indian Giver. In our evening playtimes, we could truthfully say that Dixie is an Indian Giver with her toys, for she always wants them back.

Recently I looked up the term Indian Giver. Dan and I had been reminiscing how children used to use that term, and I wondered where it came from. What I discovered was enlightening.

In the culture of the pre-colonial days here in America, the Indians had a wonderful concept of gift giving that has been lost through the remaining centuries. If a Native American liked you, he gave you one of his prized possessions. However, when you received the gift, it was understood that you would not keep it forever. When you met a new friend, you passed the gift along. Therefore, anything that you were given was not yours. You were only holding it until you could give it away again.

When the white Europeans invaded this continent, the Indians were cautious at first. But as friendships developed, the Indian gave gifts to the newcomers, expecting that they would pass the gift along to someone else and perhaps if the circle of friendship was complete, the gift would eventually return to the initial Indian Giver. Of course the newcomers did not understand the custom and kept whatever the Indian had given them. When the Indian saw the gift still in the possession of the one to whom he had given it in the first place after many moons had passed, the Indian became outraged. He would ask for the gift to be returned to him so that he could give it to someone else.

As you can see, when we children used the term Indian Giver in a derogatory sense, we did not understand where the term had originated. It would have been a much more derogatory slam if we had called the selfish child who did not want to lose his marbles a White Man Keeper rather than an Indian Giver. Still, when Dixie will not let go of her toy it sounds strange to say, "Oh, she is being a 'White Man Keeper'" but we have been known to say that she is an Indian Giver.

Fully understanding the concept behind the oft-used phrase, there could be no higher joy than to be an Indian Giver. If we would pass along every gift that we have been given to others in the manner of the ancient Americans, life would be much better.

While she may not understand the concept of the game of retrieving the ball fully, Dixie has definitely gifted us by her very presence in our lives. She certainly passes along the gift of joy, over and over again.

And when, in my relationship with God, I choose to let go of all my "toys" freely—with no tug of war and not insisting on playing for keeps—He fulfills the promise that He made in Ephesians to give us "exceedingly abundantly above all that we could ever ask or think" in return. God is perhaps the original Indian Giver who gives us gifts only so we can give them away again. One of the best gifts God has given to me is a little gray dog who reminds me of all of this!

11

Let's Go for a Ride

I have never been able to figure out how a dog knows and understands when certain events are going to take place. How, for example, does a dog know that there is a trip coming up when she sees a suitcase?

When we get our suitcases out, Dixie goes nuts! There is no other way to describe her shenanigans. She jumps on the bed, she whines, she runs to the door, she brings every toy she owns and lays them at our feet, she stands up against our legs and paws at us—all things she never does under any other circumstances. In short, she becomes an instant basket case.

In talking about this with other pet owners, I find it is not a rare phenomenon. Our daughter's job takes her out of town on lots of business trips. Her cat,

Gumbo, climbs into her suitcase when she is trying to pack it. And so, I come back to the question: How do they know? While I do not understand *how* they know, I do know *what* they know: My master is going away and I want to go along!

Traveling with a pet presents all sorts of new experiences. Sometimes it involves cleaning up a mess in the car. We had a dog before Dixie that loved to go along, no matter where we were going, but unfortunately she suffered from motion sickness. Our veterinarian told us that the best way to correct this problem was to take the dog on short jaunts so it could get used to riding. When you live on Cowpath Road in rural Champaign county, Ohio, there is no such thing as a short jaunt in the car. It is a 15 mile trip (30 miles when you count coming back!) to anywhere. We tried valiantly to help the dog learn to ride. After cleaning up several messes, we decided to bring an old plastic bowl with us in the car. Believe it or not, the poor dog learned that when she felt sick she should hang her head over the bowl. Cleanup became a lot easier, but it still was not pleasant. I developed an allergy to this dog, so she went to live with another family in our church. When we gave her to them, the bowl went with her. To this day, when they travel, they simply take the bowl along, and a bottle of water, for cleanup.

For my husband, another new experience while traveling with a dog has been frequent stopping. Our children tell their friends that their Dad could probably drive all the way from Ohio to the West Coast without stopping. Our family vacations used to consist of such questions as, "Dad, can we stop? I'm thirsty." The answer he often gave was "Swallow your own spit. We have to make it to such and such a town by 3 p.m. to stay on schedule." If you've ever seen one of Chevy Chase's vacation movies in which he is obsessed with a schedule, you've experienced traveling with Dan. Having a dog that gets "antsy" and needs to stop periodically has changed our trips rather dramatically. And, like most other changes caused by Dixie, it has been good. We now arrive at our destination less tired and achy since we have stretched our legs and walked around with her every 100 miles or so. And, like on our regular walks at home, we also notice more along the way. We stop to smell the roses.

Having a pet along can make it interesting to find a motel. Many of them will have a sign on the door to the office that states "No Pets." Others will allow you to have a pet, but only if you are willing to stay in a room designated for people who smoke. Since we are both non-smokers, I find this rule difficult to understand! Why should I have to smell tobacco on everything I touch in the room and have to air out my clothing to remove the lingering smell simply because I have a pet? But thankfully, there are hotel chains that are beginning to realize that dog lovers are among the nicest people on God's green earth, and so they are opening their doors to master and pet alike. We tend to gravitate toward these hotels even if Dixie is not traveling with us, since we enjoy meeting the people who stay there more than those in the snobby places that refuse rooms to pet owners.

Whether it is for a long trip or a short one, when we ask Dixie if she wants to go for a ride, she is always a happy pup. Unlike other pets we have had in the past, she really seems to want to see where we are going. Instead of curling up and going to sleep, she enjoys looking out the window. If possible, she wants to be on my lap in the front seat. She sits tall and stares ahead, glancing to the sides only to growl at a passing animal. She looks like a little soldier, watching the road ahead for possible mishaps. If I tire of holding her, she is banished to the back seat. Though we bring toys along, she ignores them. She places herself in the middle of the back seat with her front paws on the two armrests over the console in the front seat. In this way, she can still see where we are headed.

Our children cannot understand why Dan and I love to travel by car. They like to get to wherever they are going as soon as possible to enjoy the resort, beach, mountains, or whatever. Whenever it is possible, they fly to their destination. We fly when necessary, but much prefer traveling by car so that we can enjoy everything there is to see along the way.

On a clear day, you can make out the boundaries of farms, lakes, and towns from the air. On that same clear day in a car you can see the wonderful ways people landscape their properties, enjoy watching the boaters on lakes, and stop for a cup of coffee at "Bud's Eatery" in the little towns you pass through. Dixie does not want to miss seeing anything along the way, and neither do we.

Seeing Dixie watch every mile that passes reinforces in my mind the truth expounded in an untitled essay by an unknown author who says:

> We convince ourselves that life will be better after we get married, have a baby, then another. Then we are frustrated that the kids aren't old enough and we'll be more content when they are. After that, we're frustrated that we have teenagers to deal with. We will certainly be happy when they are out of that stage. We tell ourselves that our life will be complete when our spouse gets his or her act together, when we get a nicer car, are able to go on a nice vacation, or when we retire. The truth is, there's no better time to be happy than right now. If not now, when?

Our lives will always be filled with challenges. It's best to admit this to ourselves and decide to be happy anyway. One of my favorite quotes comes from Alfred D. Souza. He said, "For a long time it had seemed to me that life was about to begin—real life. But there was always some obstacle in the way, something to be gotten through first, some unfinished business, time still to be served, or a debt to be paid. Then life would begin. At last it dawned on me that these obstacles *were* my life."

This perspective has helped me to see that there is no way *to* happiness—happiness *is* the way. We must treasure every moment that we have and all the more because we share it with someone special. We need to keep in mind that time waits for no one. We should quit waiting until we finish school or go back to school, lose ten pounds or gain ten pounds, until we have kids or they leave the nest, until we start work or retire from work, until we get married or get divorced, until Friday night or Sunday morning, until we get a new car/home or until it is paid off, until spring, summer, fall, or winter, until we die or until we are born again and decide that there is no better time than right now to be happy. Happiness is a journey, not a destination.

We tried to teach our children this truth when they were young. We tried to take family vacations that would not only be enjoyable but educational. We visited lots of historical sites and traveled many miles.

It is true that we were tied to a much-too-full schedule on our trips, but we did find ways to enjoy the ride. There were many games of finding each letter in the alphabet on signs. (Did you know that whoever finds a "J" first almost invariably wins this game?) We sang as we rode, and our finale song was always the same. Dan and I perfected a duet of the Beatles song "Help" when we were dating in high school. We knew the kids were tired of singing when one of them said, "You two sing 'Help.'" Our rendition is corny and always brought laughter into the journey.

There was one vacation, however, in which our determination to enjoy the journey was severely challenged. Sonya was 17 and Kyer was 15. We wanted to show them America, but the only way we could afford to do so was to camp. So we headed west with our brand new tent and four bulging suitcases in an enclosed turtle-style top carrier atop our compact car. The first several days were fun, with the exception of overcrowding in the tent and a few whines about having to walk a block to the restroom. Getting our camp set up each afternoon after a long day in the rather small car usually had some heated moments. But we saw the Gateway Arch in St. Louis, the endless rolling hills of Kansas, the Grand Canyon, and Disneyland. For the most part, we were enjoying ourselves.

Then we made the joint decision to go to the studio where the TV Game Show "Password" was filmed and try to get tickets to watch the taping. We parked the car on Bob Hope Drive in the designated area, stood in a very long line, but then thoroughly enjoyed getting to watch all that went into taping the show. Our plan for that evening was to drive a short distance out of the city and camp somewhere that had a pool or a beach. As we drove along, people began to honk their horns as they passed us and point to the roof of our car. We finally realized something must be wrong and pulled to the side of the busy freeway.

Dan got out and said, "Oh no, the top carrier has come open!" I jumped out on my side to make sure nothing had come out. He was beginning to fasten the latch again when I screamed, "It's empty!"

While we had been enjoying the television show,

someone had broken into our top carrier and stolen our suitcases (which contained all our clothing) and our tent. We were absolutely stunned and sat in the car wondering what we should do. Our daughter had purchased a lot of new clothing for college to which she was headed in a few weeks., and it was now all gone. Tears began to slide down her cheeks. I was shaking from head to foot and asking, "Where will we sleep? How will we get back home?" There were not nearly enough travelers checks in the glove compartment to pay for motels. We decided that we should go back to Burbank and fill out a police report, so we exited the freeway, crossed the overpass, and headed south again. The car had never been so silent. We definitely were not enjoying this journey.

Our son had a nasty pair of sweat pants that he had worn for grass cutting, basketball, and any time he wanted to be comfortable. Just before the trip, he had taken scissors and haphazardly chopped off the legs of these pants, turning them into nasty sweat shorts. We were about half way back to the city when he muttered, "You know what? I think I was emotionally attached to those sweat shorts."

Dan, Sonya, and I exploded in uncontrollable laughter. Here we were wondering how we were going to get home and Sonya was wondering what she would wear in college, while Kyer was worrying about a pair of shorts that should have been trashed months ago.

This trip went from bad to worse. After an unsuccessful trip to the Burbank police department, we decided to drive all night if necessary to get to my brother's home in San Francisco. We were making our way up Route 5, topping the dreaded Grapevine mountain range at about midnight. The kids and I were asleep, when suddenly the car stopped. We all roused up to see what was happening only to hear a very exasperated Dan explain that we had a flat tire! I held the flashlight for him as he labored in hurricane force winds to change that tire. Trucks passed us doing 80 miles per hour and the wind they created nearly blew the little car off the jack. Our kids still refer to this as the only time they ever heard their father cuss.

In fact, when we get together and begin reminiscing over fun times, someone always brings it up. "Remember the vacation when we got robbed?" Looking back, it truly was a fun time—proof positive that if we learn to enjoy the ride like Dixie does, the journey is what it is all about.

Dixie's predecessor, Rebel, never learned to enjoy the trip. She was filled with fear of things that she encountered along the journey. She did okay as long as there was nothing extraordinary on the ride. But if she saw something she was not used to in her day to day life, she became a nervous wreck. There were three things that sent her "over the edge" while riding in a car. The first one was toll booths. Can you imagine being frightened of toll booths? We made a trip to Virginia with Rebel. Not knowing of her fear, we took the Pennsylvania turnpike part of the way. Each time we came to a booth where the toll needed to be paid, she trembled violently and whined uncontrollably. The poor dog would just be beginning to enjoy the trip again when we would encounter another toll booth. At first, we laughed. Eventually we rerouted ourselves, not being sure any little dog body could withstand the violent tremors she was experiencing.

On that same trip we discovered that Rebel had another huge fear—tunnels! As we approached a long tunnel through a mountain, I whispered, "I wonder what Rebel will do in the tunnel?"

Dan assured me that, since she was asleep, there was nothing to worry about. As soon as we entered the tunnel, Rebel mysteriously awakened and bounded over the back seat, landing squarely in my lap. She trembled so violently and whined so pitifully that as soon as we were through the tunnel we stopped to let her walk around and try to "get over it." We had thought of taking a bridge across Chesapeake Bay that tunnels under the water at the midway point. Eventually we scrapped that idea in favor of a road which would cause Rebel less stress.

The third fear Rebel was never able to overcome was of drive-thrus. She did not discriminate. She was petrified of banks as well as fast food restaurants. She even shook with fear when we stopped to pick up the mail from the rural mailbox at the road in front of our home. Something about opening the car window and pulling up alongside something just gave her the willies!

Like many people, Rebel feared anything that was unknown to her. Obviously she did not enjoy the journey. And we were told by our veterinarian at the time of her early demise that it was very possible her little system was full of open ulcers—a direct result of all the fears she was never able to overcome. If only she could have learned to enjoy the journey rather than fear it, she would have lived a longer, happier life.

Although I believe that life is what happens while you are on the journey, there is an interesting phenomenon that Dixie and other animals all seem to experience. Whether the car ride has been just 15 miles into town to drop something off at the post office or a 2,000 mile vacation, how do they know when they are almost home? When we turn the last corner onto our beloved Cow Path Road, she snaps to attention, her tail begins to wag, and sometimes she even whines in anticipation. Though she has enjoyed the journey, she is always so happy to be home.

When our kids were small, my mother taught them the same nonsensical nursery rhyme she had taught to me as a child. When the car pulled into the driveway she would often say, "To market, to market, to buy a fat pig. Home again, home again, jiggety jig. To market, to market, to buy a fat hog. Home again, home again, jiggety jog." These were always the final 30 words of every long trip. Even now, my husband will often say the last six words of the rhyme as we pull into our garage.

It is my simple hope that my life can mirror Dixie's in my enjoyment of the journey. And when I come to the end of this life, I know (through faith in Jesus) that I will be wagging my tail (figuratively, of course) in joyful anticipation of being "home again, home again, jiggety jog."

12

Idiosyncrasies

D r. James Dobson wrote a best selling book on raising children entitled *Dare to Discipline*. In that book, Dr. Dobson described the difference between what he called "strong willed children" and "compliant children." Not having a Ph.D. behind my name (or any other letters for that matter), I do not know whether these two basic personalities exist in the animal kingdom or not. But I do know that some of our pets have seemed to be obstinate and bull-headed to the point of being nearly untrainable. Perhaps they would be labeled as strong willed by someone more learned than me. If the labels do fit the animals of the world, then Dixie would be called the most compliant of all dogs I have ever known.

When guests visit our home and meet her, they invariably ask how we trained her. We get comments such as, "That is the most well behaved dog I have ever seen." Perhaps the highest praise we have heard yet came from an older lady in our congregation who was at a committee meeting in our living room. When the meeting was about to break up, she said, "I normally don't even like dogs—but Dixie could come and live with me any time." As typical old-time farmers, she and her husband have never had an "indoor" pet. At the end of another meeting her husband said, "If you ever need a place to leave that little dog for a few days, we would be glad to have it." And so the question often arises. How did we train her?

The answer is simple. To a large extent, we didn't! She seemed to come to us with an inborn sense of "right and wrong," already knowing all the little doggy rules. And for those that she did not know, it only took a gentle reprimand a couple of times for her to catch on. Like the compliant child Dr. Dobson discusses in his writings, Dixie seems to want to please us and making us happy seems to be her main goal in life.

This is not to say that she has never needed discipline, but she has been very easy to discipline. In fact, we have to be very careful to correct her minor misbehaviors without breaking her spirit in the process.

We first realized what a compliant little dog she is back when we were still consulting the oft-mentioned puppy book. In this book, the authors went into a lengthy discussion about how dogs are basically pack animals and will rule the home if allowed. The book said that the dog will think it is "top dog" and all the humans are members of its pack. It said it was very important to banish this idea from the puppy's little brain early in its training. To make the puppy know that you are the master, it said, you must teach the puppy to roll over on its back and stay in that position until you tell it to move. One of the funny idiosyncrasies about Dixie's little personality is that the very first time I ever raised my voice at her she plopped over onto her back with all four feet extended up in the air. It took me by such surprise that I giggled, "Look at this, Dan." While we laughed, she remained in that position, rolling her big brown eyes as if to say, "Please don't beat me!"

Dixie is now two years old and she still does it. One of her favorite toys is an empty plastic pop bottle. We remove the paper, screw the lid on tight, and toss it to her. She throws it into the air herself, catching it on the way down. She gets the neck of the bottle in her mouth and races all through the house carrying it. She loves her pop bottles, which makes me wonder why we bother to purchase toys for our pets when discarded trash can be so much fun. When she tires a bit, she lies down and works and works until she gets the lid off the bottle. The lid is a bit too small for her to safely chew, so when I see that she has removed the lid I simply raise my voice a little bit and say, "Dixie, stop." Immediately she rolls over on her back. I take the lid away from her and toss it in the trash. Sometimes I forget to tell her that it is okay and will find her still lying on her back waiting for me to give her permission to get up when I return from the wastebasket. If she could talk, I am certain she would be saying, "I am so sorry. I don't know why I always take the lid off. Don't be mad at me. Please forgive me. I'll try to be good."

Dixie is not, however, a perfect dog. She has her moments. The reader will remember the Christmas bear incident. There have been two other offenses of note in her young life. The first occurred when we had only had her about a month. She was so tiny, and I did not yet trust her potty habits. So whenever she "disappeared" from view I would go on a search mission. One time, just as I got up from my chair to see what she was into, she came walking very slowly into the hallway, backwards! The reason she was walking backwards was that she was gently pulling toilet paper. How I wished I had a camcorder rolling! America's Funniest Home Videos would have had a new winner. Not only was it amazing that she was "T.P.-ing" the house, she was tugging so gently on the roll that she had rounded two corners and traversed about 20 feet with the end of the roll in her mouth, yet it had not torn off the dispenser in the bathroom.

My reaction was automatic. "Dixie," I exclaimed. "What are you doing?"

She dropped the toilet paper and rolled over on her back. I couldn't even reprimand her; I was laughing so hard. I just picked her up and loved her. Here was a girl after my own heart. Some of my most exciting and fun moments as a teenager had been tossing rolls of toilet paper high into the trees and twisting it into wild contortions in every direction. I was convinced back then that this was a rare art form. Dixie had been studiously trying to decorate her new domain. As I carried her, I re-rolled the toilet paper onto the roll and gently told her that she should never do this again. Dan and I worked together to make sure the end of the paper was not hanging at a height she could reach. It never happened again. I have never told Dixie, but I am a little disappointed that she gave up so easily. Even when forced to go the next day and pull down all the T.P. from the house we had decorated with such abandon the previous night, I never gave up. But obviously, I am not a compliant child.

Other than the Christmas bear, Dixie has always known not to play with any of my other bears. But, there was a problem near the bears. Two of my favorites that get a lot of comment from guests are a grandma and granddaughter set of bears. They sit in a one foot high, green, corduroy overstuffed chair. Grandma bear has a book on her lap and granddaughter bear has an inquisitive look on her face as she stares up at her grandma. This little combination always reminds me of the hours our daughter, Sonya, spent sitting beside my mother in a big arm chair as Grandma read. When Sonya was about six years old, she crawled up beside Grandma but the fit was getting snug. She innocently looked at my pleasantly plump mother and exclaimed, "One of us is too big!" In memory of this incident that still brings a smile to all of us, I arranged these two bears in the same way. The chair has a matching green corduroy ottoman in front of it. After the unfortunate early demise of Dixie's predecessor, Rebel, I found a tiny ceramic schnauzer just the right size. So there is a little dog perched atop the ottoman, sound asleep.

Or, perhaps I should say, it *was* sound asleep until Dixie came into our lives. Three times that little ceramic schnauzer, that looks so much like Dixie, came up missing. Upon searching, sure enough, we found it in Dixie's toy box. We scolded her and told her that this little dog does not belong to her and she should leave it alone. She rolled onto her back, as usual but followed me and looked longingly at the little knick-knacks as I replaced it on the Grandma bear's ottoman. Her eyes were saying, "I never got to have children of my own. Why can't I adopt this one?" She never chewed the hard little dog but only licked it. After the three reprimands, she has never played with the little dog again, but she does look longingly at it. Personally, I think our Dixie Lee would have made a wonderful mother.

I was determined that Dixie would not be like some rude dogs and jump all over people who came to visit us. I also did not want her to bark uncontrollably. Since both of her bloodlines (poodles and schnauzers) have a predominant "yapping" gene, I was determined that she would control this tendency. People tend to stop into the parsonage pretty often, so we kept a rolled up newspaper near the door. Why she is so frightened of a rolled up newspaper is anyone's guess, for we have never actually hit her with it. We simply smacked our hand or the floor near her with it and said, "No, Dixie. Stay back!" Or "No, Dixie. Don't bark!" I could tell by the way she cowered that someone in her past (perhaps her mommy dog?) had told her that humans have a weapon of mass destruction called a rolled up newspaper. As a result of this action taken early in her life, Dixie never barks. Correction—I guess I need to back up. She hardly ever barks.

The head deacon in our church is a wonderful man named Daryl. However, from the first day he saw Dixie, he has barked at her at every encounter. He has a beard and moustache which is nearly identical to Dixie's in color, and he loves to torment her by getting down at her level and barking at her. I tried valiantly to keep her from barking back at him, but then decided that it was a bit much to expect a dog who is being barked at not to bark back. And so, one of Dixie's idiosyncrasies is that she only barks at one person— Daryl!

Oftentimes there is activity at the church which sits next door to our home. And the fellowship hall of the church is the basement of the parsonage, so there are many meetings which take place in the basement. Even though the fellowship hall has outside entrances and Dixie may not even see the people enter, the noise drifts upward and we can tell that something is happening downstairs. Can you imagine the chaos a barking dog would create with these circumstances? She growls to let us know that she hears or sees something strange. But as soon as we tell her it is okay, she calms down and ignores whatever is happening. But when she barks and carries on uncontrollably, whether she is in the backyard or looking out the doorway of our house, we know that Daryl has arrived. He is a fun-loving man and will hide from us, trying to get Dixie in trouble. But it has happened so often that his cover is blown. When she barks, we just say, "Where is Daryl?" and she leads us to him. The odd thing is—in spite of all his teasing, Dixie loves Daryl. I think, because of his bushy gray/white beard, she thinks they are related.

Is it cruel of me not to allow Dixie to bark? Isn't that the only way a dog knows to communicate? I have wrestled with this idea.

We visited a large dog breeder's business one time. It was unbelievably quiet, considering the fact that there were nearly 100 dogs there in various size kennels and runs. Suddenly I realized that the dogs were opening their mouths, but only hoarse squeaks were emerging. All of the adult dogs had been de-barked. I was outraged.

I asked the veterinarian that I worked for about the procedure, and he replied that it is a relatively simple operation. When I asked him if he had ever done it, he hung his head and I think I saw his eyes well up. "One time," he replied. "It was a magnificent German shepherd. The little lady had purchased him for a watchdog. He did his job too well, I guess, so she begged me to de-bark him. It is the only operation I have ever performed that made me sick to my stomach. The dog came through fine—but I determined that day that I would never do that again."

From time to time I remembered his words and

wondered if I might have harmed Dixie's little psyche when I told her not to bark. I could envision her on a doggy version of the Oprah show, or Maury, or (heaven forbid) Jerry Springer, confessing to all dogs everywhere, "The reason I am a mass murderer is that my master would never allow me to bark!"

Dixie relieved my worries one evening when Dan was gone to a meeting. Dixie heard something outside and set up a howl that would have scared off the bravest burglar. I told her to stop barking and went to check that all three doors were locked and dead-bolted. As soon as she knew we were safe, she stopped barking. And so, it seems, this gentle little dog understands more than I give her credit for. It is not that she feels abused that she is not allowed to bark. It is just that she knows when and where barking is appropriate—at things that go bump in the night! And, of course, at Daryl!

Another of Dixie's idiosyncrasies involves her posture. Much of the time, she stands with her back legs crossed. And just as often, she has her right front paw in the air. She looks remarkably like a little girl in kindergarten who desperately needs to use the restroom. We have no idea why she stands this way, but sometimes I find myself putting her outside to do her business when she has no business to do.

When we do put her outside, she displays another anomaly of her little personality. She never goes down the steps and into the yard without stopping on the top step to survey her territory. She slowly turns her head from left to right, looking carefully at every corner of the yard. It is as if she thinks she needs to check for invaders before she descends from her balcony. Dan calls this her "king of the world" stance.

We have just experienced one of the worst winters on record in Ohio. The snow was almost as deep as the chain link fence that surrounds Dixie's domain—our back yard. When I put her out and the snow was deep, she would frolic over to the fence-line and assume her royal stance atop the mountain of snow. It reminded me of endless games of "King of the Hill" I had participated in my childhood winters. If she had only known, Dixie could have easily stepped across the fence at that time and been free to explore the world outside the enclosure. However, I never told her that she could, so Miss Compliant never tried.

Isn't it hilarious that every pet comes with inbred idiosyncrasies? We are thankful that Dixie's are all rather cute and endearing. In fact, even these rather strange habits and pieces of her personality puzzle remind me of my relationship with a loving heavenly Father.

You see, even pastors and pastors' wives come with inbred oddities. Some congregants put us up on pedestals and get hurt when we suddenly topple at their feet. I am thankful that God loves us, no matter what we do that seems strange.

For example, Dan is a first class, full blown, dyed in the wool, slightly insane sports nut, and I knew this when I married him. After all, we had gone together all through junior high and high school. When other girls were being taken to lovely romantic dinners, our dates had often been to sporting events. Deep down, I thought this would change a bit after we got married. Silly me!

As for me, I am a first class, full blown, dyed in the wool, slightly insane shopping nut! There is no activity that is more fun for me than roaming the mall in search of bargains. Sometimes during our dating years (on the rare occasion when there was no sporting event we could attend), Dan asked me what I wanted to do. I think he dreaded the answer. "Let's go to the mall," I always said with a grin. He probably hoped that this would change a bit after we married. Silly him!

We have learned to adjust. After 34 years of marriage and many unnecessary arguments on these two subjects, we now compromise. I go willingly with him to see the Cincinnati Reds play baseball if he goes willingly with me to get a new pair of shoes. He goes willingly with me to a flea market if I will allow him full control of the TV remote on Saturday afternoons. I am embarrassed when I remember all the times we tried to change each other's inbred idiosyncrasies. How thankful I am that God never does.

I am also thankful that our congregation has learned to accept and love Dan and me in spite of our personality quirks. Many of the farmers in our church have never watched a ball game of any type at any time in their lives. Yet, they smile indulgently as Dan uses illustrations from the world of sports in his sermons. Many of the women in our church dread a trip to the mall worse than a trip to the doctor. Yet, they chuckle as I tell them excitedly of purchasing something during the Clover Day sales, saving 50% because of the sale, another 25% with a coupon, and 10% because I found that the skirt was missing a button. Not all congregations are so patient with their pastoral family.

During his sessions of giving marital counseling, Dan has seen how the arguments that bring a couple to him are often over simple idiosyncrasies in their different personalities. Many of the traits that seem so cute and endearing during the dating years become horrible obstacles to be overcome in a marriage. It is at times like these that he reminds the couple that God accepts them as they are, with all of their little habits and oddities. The trick to a lasting relationship is to decide what is worth barking about, when to roll over in submission, and how to accept each others' quirks.

When the couple refuses to compromise, Dixie stands tall as a perfect example of someone with idiosyncrasies that everyone loves. Perhaps her most endearing trait is that she wants desperately to make us happy. If only we could learn to be like her in all our relationships!

13

Lost Dog?

After speaking at a ladies retreat last year, I returned home extremely tired but also filled with the Lord's blessings. I engage in these experiences, praying that I might be a blessing to the people, and that God will speak through me to the needs in their hearts and lives. More often than not, it is me who receives a blessing. God works through the people to reach my needs and I am grateful. These were my feelings as I entered the house that rainy evening and received greetings in the usual order—Dixie first, and then Dan.

After giving me a warm hug and kiss, Dan watched as I knelt to scratch Dixie's head and let her give me another quick "kiss." "We could have had a tragedy last night," he said.

"What?" I asked, still petting the dog.

"Well, I put Dixie outside before bedtime like always. I was watching TV and went to let her in about ten minutes later, but she wasn't there!" he explained. Picking her up and cuddling her, I waited to hear the rest with a lump in my throat.

"I called and called," he said. "Then I turned on all the outside lights and realized she was gone. Someone had left one of the gates open."

By this time I was near tears. "What did you do? How did you find her?"

"Well, I got my shoes on and ran through the gate calling her name. Thankfully, she was just standing at the edge of the cornfield, looking confused, and came to me right away when she saw me."

I carried Dixie into the living room and held her tightly while Dan brought in my suitcase and other retreat paraphernalia. As I stated before, I was tired and yet felt extremely blessed by God. Perhaps that is why the emotions swept over me so quickly. By the time he had unloaded the car, he found me holding Dixie close and quietly crying.

"Honey, what's wrong? She didn't get lost. I checked all the gates. She's here; I'm here. You're home! Why are you crying?"

"Oh Danny—what if she had gotten into that huge cornfield? What if you hadn't found her? What if when I came home tonight you had said she was gone? Lost forever? Is it possible to love a little dog too much? What if—?" By now, I was sobbing in his embrace, with Dixie between us.

He quietly reassured me, "She didn't get lost. She didn't go into the corn. But, if she had—well, we would have searched. We would have called for her. We would never have given up until we found her."

I was immediately transported back in time over 40 years and approximately 60 miles to the north when I was a little fourth grade girl who lived with her Mom, Dad, big brothers, and our dog Tippy on Atlantic Avenue in Lima, Ohio. Tippy was of mixed doggy heritage, but her dominant features were those of a beagle. Her features were matched by a beagle's characteristic need to hunt. Every time that it was at all possible, Tippy would break free from confinement (whether a fence, chain, or rope) and begin to run in happy abandon with her nose on the ground. She periodically howled with glee when she picked up the scent of—who knows? We lived right in the middle of town, so was it be a squirrel or a confused rabbit? Whichever one it was, she ran after it like an Olympian chasing a gold medal. She loved to run. Many times we found her rope still attached to the clothesline on one end, but the other end was broken and she was gone. We kids worried, but she always came back. Sometimes in the winter, the pads of her feet were cut from running on jagged ice. In the summer, she lay in the shade and panted for hours upon her return.

One day, however, she did not return. My brother David had two years seniority on me, so while he combed the neighborhood calling for Tippy, I was sent to bed. I remember crying and praying that God would keep her safe and bring her home. About an hour later, I heard Dad whistle. He could split the air with a whistle that was heard for several blocks. We kids knew that when he whistled it was our job to shout "Coming" and be on the porch in short order. When Dad whistled that night, it sounded as if David's voice was breaking when he answered "Coming." I heard both Mom and Dad assuring David that he should come to bed. "She'll probably be on the porch when we wake up in the morning," they said.

She wasn't! David got ready for school, quickly swallowed his eggs and bacon in huge bites that morning, and explained, "I have a half hour. I'm gonna look for Tippy!" as he raced out the door. He came close to being late for school, but arrived, hot and sweaty, just as the last bell rang. I was in my fourth grade line, about to enter the building. He shook his head dejectedly at me from the sixth grade line, and I knew his search again had been in vain.

Our lives took on a horrible sameness for days. As long as it was light enough in the evenings, he and I would both search. We had a system—we covered the blocks around our home, calling her name at each house. We walked through the alleys that cut through the blocks both directions, checking open garages, sheds, and searching along hedges and fences.

"What if she is hurt?" I asked him more than once.

"She'll be okay," he'd respond—but his eyes didn't look as if he believed himself. I had to be home by dark, so he walked with me back to the house to retrieve his flashlight and went back out again.

There was a live morning radio talk show broadcast

in our town. The hostess' name was Easter Straker, and the name of the program was Easter's Parade. In Lima, Ohio, this morning radio anchor person was our Oprah Winfrey, Dr. Phil, Martha Stewart, Jane Pauley, and Phil Donahue all rolled into one. I remember how people complained that she could talk more and say less than any other woman on earth.

After David had searched from daylight till dark for a week for our beloved dog, Mom grew desperate. She finally called the radio station during a commercial and asked to speak to Easter Straker. Much to her surprise, the woman herself came to the phone.

Mom described the situation in a clear and succinct manner. Within moments, Easter was back on the air. Mom remembers that she said something like this:

"Now, listen up—all of you out there in radio-land! I just had a phone call from a very distraught mother who lives on Atlantic Avenue. It seems this family has lost their dog. It is a black, brown, and white beagle mix who answers to the name of Tippy. The dog is a female who has been spayed and is about a year old. This woman has a 12 year old son who is beside himself with fear and grief over losing this little dog. She said that he is walking the streets calling, 'Heeeeee-re Tippy' before school every morning and after school every evening until it is so late that he has to go to bed. She said that he doesn't want to take time to eat and just keeps saying, 'We have to find her. She could be hurt.' So, how about it, Lima-land? Has anyone seen a dog matching this description? Let's help this little guy find his pet dog. If you have any knowledge of this dog's whereabouts, please call me!"

Late that afternoon, Mom received a phone call. She spoke excitedly into the receiver and then whispered something to Dad. He went to the porch and whistled. Quickly he and David hopped in our 1952 car and drove nearly a mile into a poorer section of the city. I think they did not want me to know what was going on, fearing this might not be the answer for which we had prayed.

Maybe a half hour passed, or maybe it was only minutes. All I remember is being on the front porch with Mom when the car rounded the corner, horn honking, and David waving excitedly. I knew in a flash that Tippy was with them in the car.

Dad carried a box carefully into the living room, and a cut and bruised Tippy was curled in a heap on a blanket. "She had been hit by a car on Elm Street," he explained as we knelt on the floor petting her. "She pulled herself up onto a porch and a poor family has been caring for her ever since." As an aside to Mom, he whispered, "I tried to give them some money, but they wouldn't take it."

His words were not heard at first, for Tippy was crying! She howled, barked, whined, and howled some more. She tried to wag her long tail, but we could tell every movement hurt. The noises coming from her throat were heart-rending. Of course, all of us were crying. And when I say all of us, I mean ALL—including Tippy. Huge tears rolled down her face as she howled her gratitude to a family (especially one little boy) who cared enough to search for a hopelessly lost dog.

The whole scene was vividly etched into my mind. And so, holding Dixie close, I asked Dan, "Did I ever tell you about the time Tippy got lost?" He nodded his head with a tender smile on his face.

"Yes, honey—but Dixie did not get lost. You look exhausted. Why don't you take a hot shower? Then we'll go to bed—all three of us."

When I crawled into our bed that evening, so thankful that Dixie was still here with us, I was reminded of a passage of scripture in Luke 15 when Jesus told three stories to a group of people who were gathered. The first one tells of a man who had 100 sheep, and when one got lost, he left the 99 and went in search of the lost one. The second story tells of a woman who had ten coins but misplaced one. Jesus says she would "light a lamp and look in every corner of the house and sweep every nook and cranny until she finds it" (New Living Translation).

The third story is the often quoted story of the Prodigal Son. People who never darken the door of a church know that a prodigal son is one who has left home and turned his back on his parents' lifestyle, preferring to "sow his wild oats." Eventually, the Lord tells us, the son became tired of the way he was living and longed to return home. He realized he had sinned against his father but determined in his heart that he would ask forgiveness and try to make things right, so he began the long journey back. The thing that always amazes me anew each time I read this chapter in Luke is that Jesus says in verse 20, "And while he was still a long distance away, his father saw him coming. Filled with love and compassion, he ran to his son, embraced him, and kissed him" (New Living Translation).

In my mind's eye, I can envision the tears that were shed for this son who came back to his home. I believe it was similar to the welcome Tippy received that night long ago on Atlantic Avenue. She had wandered away of her own free will, and then she got to a place where she wanted to come home, but her injuries prevented her from doing so. With great love, David and I searched. Mom made a phone call. Dad drove the car. And eventually all of us were rejoicing.

When people wander away from their heavenly Father, I believe He lovingly goes out and searches for them. He goes to where they are and never gives up. He lets them hear sermons, arranges for them to meet His servants who will help them, and goes out again and again calling their name. And, eventually, there is great celebration mingled with tears when the wandering person is found. Jesus describes the scene in Luke 15:10 when He says, "There is joy in the presence of God's angels when even one sinner repents" (New Living Translation).

All these thoughts and more crowded in my mind that night, which was by the way, the first night we ever allowed Dixie to sleep with us!

14

Come Bringing Gifts

When Dixie was a puppy, I am afraid we made a big mistake. Nearly every time we went to the store and came to the Pet Food aisle, we purchased a surprise for our new little friend. It did not take this smart little dog long to realize that when we came in the door with many bags, it often meant that she was going to get a new toy.

Dan told me that I was going to spoil her rotten. "But it is so much fun to give her something new," was my quick reply. He would just grin and nod his head.

When we give Dixie a new toy, the routine is always the same. She gets so excited that she can hardly stand the waiting. Dan makes it worse by telling her, "Look Dixie! A new toy for you!" while he is cutting the tags off it. By the time he is ready to give it to her, she has run several circles around his feet, whined, jumped around in ecstasy, and begged in every way possible.

And then comes the fun of watching her investigate the new item! She walks around the toy warily, never taking her eye off it, stalking it like a lioness with its prey. She leans forward from a safe distance and nudges it with her nose, as if it might attack her without any provocation. Eventually she reaches out her right front paw and barely touches it, always jumping back—just in case it is something that can hurt her. This rigmarole goes on for several minutes until she finally gets the nerve to pick it up in her mouth.

At this point, she begins to play with complete abandon. I don't think she even knows whether we are around, so absorbed is she with her new plaything. She chews it, sniffs it, bats it across the floor with her paw, picks it up and tosses it above her head, and races through the house carrying it. This will go on for hours until, inevitably, she will fall asleep with her head or her paw on the new item. It makes no difference whether it is hard or soft, a rawhide chew stick or a squeaky ball—she is simply thrilled to have something new to play with. Can you see why I like to buy toys for her?

But Dan is correct. I probably overdid it when she was a puppy because to this day, when either of us comes in from the store, she sits at our feet, wiggles, bats her eyelashes, and very clearly says, "What did you bring me?"

Of all household jobs, the one I detest the most is grocery shopping, because it is so hard to think of anything different to purchase. The lines are often crowded, and invariably, I get behind someone who is writing a check, using a million coupons, or needs a price check on several hard-to-find items. By the time I get home from this chore, I am usually not a happy person to be around. Oftentimes when I am unsacking groceries and putting them away I will say, "Dixie, I did not get anything for you this time. Now go play."

In typical Dixie fashion, she just looks a little sad and goes to find her bear. She never pouts or carries a grudge. She never says, "It has been months since I had a new chew stick." She just accepts that this is not the time, but she also never gives up. The next time either of us comes in the door carrying a sack, she will be there—always hoping.

When I was a little girl, I was extremely close to my Dad. Mom is my best friend on earth—but what I shared with Dad was something rare. I suppose part of it was because I was the youngest of five children and the only girl. After four sons, I suppose I was something unique.

I wish I could say I was a perfect little lady. It is much closer to the truth to say that I was (am?) a bit of a "tomboy." I have always blamed this, in part, to growing up with my brothers. But part of it, too, is because I always wanted to be with Dad.

When I was small, he drove from Atlantic Avenue out into the country to purchase fresh milk, and I always wanted to ride along. This was in the days long before mandatory car seats or even seatbelts. So there I was, at the age of two, riding along with Dad to get milk. It was on those trips that he taught me to spell Saratoga. Our Chrysler had the model name written in chrome letters on the glove compartment. He taught me what each letter was, and then he would tell me to spell it. Once I had learned to recognize the letters, he would have me turn around on the seat and hide my eyes against the upholstery. Then he would say, "Spell Saratoga." I was probably the only child alive who could spell that word before I could even spell my own name.

Dad had pitched baseball in high school and loved the sport. None of my four brothers was ever very interested in the game, but I was. I had my own mitt and Dad spent hours teaching me which way to turn the glove. "Now this one is going to be to your left. Don't move to your left. Just reach across your body and turn your glove over to catch it."

Our family went camping for two weeks every summer at Gun Lake in Michigan. We had a boat and spent many hours in water sports, all of us learning to ski on that lake. My favorite memory of our camping vacations, however, is one that only Dad and I shared. He always rose early, almost at daybreak. I would hear him starting the Coleman camp stove, and soon I smelled the coffee. The sleeping bag was warm and I was comfortable, but something better than warmth and comfort called my name. I hastily pulled on jeans and a hooded sweatshirt, socks, and shoes. I quietly left the tent, ran across the campground to use the outhouse, and then rushed back to our campsite.

Dad was always sitting on the end of the picnic table, drinking his coffee and smiling at me. "Morning, Dad!" I always said and he always replied, "Are you ready to go?" Nodding to him, I ran over to the boat, untied the rope, and tossed it across the deck as he started the engine—we were off on our morning boat ride.

I don't remember talking much on those rides. Often we drove through what I called "fog," but Dad said it was steam caused by the temperature of the air being colder than that of the water. When I was very small, he would pat his lap and I would climb up on his knee and drive! I don't think I even knew that his hands were also on the wheel. Then, as I grew, he would slide across the seat and say, "She's all yours!" We avoided the places where there were groups of fisherman, for we always liked to go fast. With me behind the wheel, he'd say, "Open her up!" It felt like we were flying across the water. It seemed as though we went so much faster when I drove than when he did. All too soon, we headed back to camp. As we pulled into the channel, we could smell bacon frying. Mom was up and about and I had chores to do—but I had begun my day on the boat with my Dad!

On those camping expeditions, we always closed our day with a campfire. We searched the nearby woods for pieces of wood throughout the day, and as soon as it began to get dark, we started the fire. Dad added wood when necessary to keep it burning, and we all sat in a circle till very late at night. Our favorite campfire activity was singing. We sang nonsense songs like "John Jacob Jingleheimer Smith" and "I've Got Sixpence." We sang Sunday School choruses and the old hymns of the church, ballads, love songs, and cowboy songs. We sang songs of America, and all of us know every word to each of the songs honoring the Marines, Air Force, Navy, and Army to this day. During these evening song times, Dad played his guitar and there were some songs that he always sang alone. He had a rich, full bass voice that was often compared to that of the great George Beverly Shea, so we all loved to hear him sing. Our song time always ended the same way when one of us kids would say, "Sing 'Old Shep,' Dad."

We all knew the words and could have sung along, but it was silently understood that this was Dad's song. Besides, he was never far into the lyrics of Red Foley's old song until there were tears dripping off all our faces. My older brothers were remembering Smoky and King and dogs I had never known, who like Old Shep, had gone on to their eternal reward. David and I were thinking of Tippy (who was being boarded at home in Ohio), and wondering what we would ever do if we had to face her demise.

When the song ended and the tears had been wiped away and noses had been blown, someone was sure to say, "Raelene—it's time for you to go to bed." And so, my camping days began with Dad on the boat and ended with him singing that lovely old song about a beloved dog.

After our vacation was over and we were back home, Dad always left for work before the rest of us arose in the morning. Mom got into the habit of packing his lunch the night before in a silver metal lunch box, which he and Mom always referred to as his "bucket." When I was in elementary school, I would periodically write a note to my Dad and secretly put it in his bucket. The notes were almost identical and usually said, "I love you Dad. Will you bring me something? Raelene."

The next day I eagerly waited for Dad to get home from work. He always grinned and told me to look in his bucket. Sometimes it was a roll of thin wafer candies and other times it was a box of pink, black, and white licorice flavored ones. I suppose there were times when Dad brought all of us kids something in his bucket, but the times I remember most vividly are the ones when I asked him to bring me something and he did it, just for me.

The last time I remember Dad bringing me something in his bucket was when I was older. Mom was in the hospital with pneumonia. My oldest brother and his family had moved to California, and another brother was living on the other side of our state. I was a teenager. After he had returned from visiting Mom in the hospital one school night, Dad allowed me to stay up late and watch the old black and white Spencer Tracy movie, "Father of the Bride." I think he was worried about Mom and missing my brothers. I saw a tear in his eye at the point in the movie where the daughter tells her father, "A son is a son till he gets him a wife. A daughter is a daughter all of her life." After we had gone to bed that night, I got up and wrote that little poem on a piece of paper. I could hear him snoring, so I sneaked out to the kitchen and put that note in his bucket. He never mentioned it to me, but the next day after he came home from work I found a box of licorice candies on my desk.

Was I spoiled by my father? Perhaps, but I do know this—I was loved.

Is Dixie spoiled? Perhaps, but I do know she is loved.

Gary Chapman wrote the best-selling Christian counseling book on the five different love languages. He suggests that if husbands and wives know which love language makes their spouse feel loved and then they put it into practice, marriages can be greatly improved. The love languages that Mr. Chapman identifies are: quality time, words of affirmation, gifts, acts of service, and physical touch. I am somewhat embarrassed to admit that my love language is—you guessed it—gifts.

Thankfully, my husband realizes this. He knows that if he is gone overnight I will be waiting with open arms when he comes in the door. But he also knows that among my first words will be, "What did you bring me?" I am just like Dixie, sitting there wiggling, waiting to see what surprise will come out of the sack for me.

Unlike Dixie, however, if the answer is "Nothing," I pout! I know it is immature. I know I should outgrow it, but somehow I continue to do it. Far be it from Dan to ever say to me, "I didn't get you anything this time. Now go play with whatever I brought you the last time."

They say that when a girl has a wonderful relationship with her father, she marries someone just like him. In many ways, Dan is a lot like my father. He loves sports. He loves me. And, I fear, he spoils me with gifts (but don't tell him!).

As I think back across the years, I realize that it was not the candies that were the gift that I looked forward to as a child. It was not learning to spell Saratoga on the rides to the farm where Dad bought milk. It was not getting to drive the boat on those cold camping mornings that got me out of a warm sleeping bag. It was not listening to him sing a song about a dog at the evening campfire. The real gift was Dad! What I wouldn't give to be able to spend some time with him again—but he has been in heaven for nearly 16 years. If I could see him, I wouldn't ask, "What did you bring me?" I would just enjoy being with him.

When Dan has been gone to a conference for several days, it is not really the teddy bear or the book that he brings me that I look forward to. The real gift is my husband.

In Mark 10, Peter speaks to Jesus. Like me, Peter seemed to want gifts. He says, "See, we have left all and followed You." The implied question is, "What are we going to get out of it?" Or, in Dixie's language, "What did you bring me?"

Jesus lovingly assures Peter that no one who has left house or brothers or sisters or father or mother or wife or children or lands for His sake and the Gospel will go unrewarded. He promises that His disciples will receive anything they have given up in this life a hundredfold, and in the future—eternal life. Peter may have been pouting at that point and wondering whether sacrifice for God was worth it but later on he seems to have learned the answer. In the second epistle Peter wrote, he shares that it was not gifts he needed— it was Jesus! He proclaims that "His divine power has given us everything we need for life and godliness through our knowledge of him who called us by his own glory and goodness" (2 Pet. 1:3).

I just returned from shopping. Dixie sat and watched as I unloaded the sacks. She seems to be slowly growing wiser. I know she would have been excited if I had given her something new, but she doesn't seem to get quite so hyper in anticipation. I think she has learned that it is not so much the gift that she wants, but the giver. It is my prayer that I, too, will learn this lesson.

15

Smears on the Window

One of my favorite pastimes is rearranging the furniture in our living room. Dan has often said that he is afraid to sit down in a chair in the dark in our home, for fear the chair is no longer in the spot he remembered. I like to change the location of everything about once a month. However, since last summer, my creativity has been a bit stymied.

In the arrangement I put together then, the large armchair was in front of the picture window. I placed the matching ottoman to the side of the chair, saying that we could simply pull it out in front of the chair when we wanted to use it and slide it back out of the way when we were not sitting there. "Back out of the way" meant placing the big footstool directly under the picture window.

Can you guess what happened? Dixie claimed the ottoman as her spot from which she can view her "kingdom," i.e. the vast expanse of yard, church, cemetery, and Cow Path road to be seen outside. She spends at least 12 of every 24 hours on the footrest, always watching.

There are two small problems associated with this placement of the furniture. First, I do not have the heart to change the furniture around in a way which would take the window seat away from Dixie. And second, the window is always dirty! There is a distinct smear running the width of the ottoman, just at the level of Dixie's nose. My step-dad has begun to sing "How much is that doggy in the window?" whenever he comes. Congregants expect to see Dixie at her post and worry if she is not there when they drive by the parsonage. For love of this little dog, my life has changed in two ways. I have found ways to arrange the furniture which always keep the ottoman near the window, and several times a week I can be seen with window cleaner and paper towels, trying to clean off the seemingly permanent nose smudges on the glass.

During the winter months we try to preserve heat and often pull the heavily insulated drapes until they are nearly closed. We used to close them entirely, but this past winter Dixie took it as a personal affront to her ability to watch for invaders if we did. And so we left them open over a space of about a foot of the window, right at Dixie's spot.

One day I was in the back of the house when she began to whine in a tone I had never heard before, somewhere between a howl and a cry. I ran to the living room to see if she had hurt herself in some way, but she was on the stool looking across the road. Her body was completely tense and her tail was flashing in a million-mile-per-hour blur. She continued to make the funny noise, glancing at me and then back across the road. When I followed her gaze I saw a gorgeous red fox sitting atop the stone wall around the cemetery. Its auburn-colored coat stood out in stark contrast to the white expanse of snow that had blanketed our part of the country for several weeks.

I patted Dixie on the back and said, "Oh, it's a fox!"

I am sure she understood, for she whined back that he must be a distant cousin to her and shouldn't she run out and get acquainted? I picked her up and loved her, explaining that while he looked like he wanted to play, there was a distinct possibility he could hurt her.

We watched together for several minutes. It was as if the fox were taunting her with his freedom. He ran back and forth on the stone wall, then sat and stared at us for a bit, and then ran some more. Eventually, the fox got bored with the game, but it took Dixie several minutes to believe that this potential friend had run on to other pursuits.

She has had similar experiences with squirrels and birds. In fact, it was a whine from Dixie that alerted me to the first robin of the new spring the other day. I was glad that I saw it—a sign of hope, a promise of better weather coming.

Every evening, Dixie has a few minutes of agony when our nearest neighbor, about a mile away, walks her huge rottweiler on the Cow Path. I know she would dearly love to go out and meet this neighbor, but we always tell her that it would take one look at her and say, "Hmm....lunch!" I doubt Dixie would be more than three bites for that huge monstrosity of a dog. But from behind the safety of the picture window, Dixie emits some fierce sounding grunts and growls.

Since Cow Path Road is so deserted, Dixie often falls asleep waiting to see anything worthwhile as she sits on the ottoman. We have found her with her head on the window sill, gently snoring, many times. But she continues her sentry duty.

When I am in the study or in the back of the house, I can almost always tell by the amount of commotion she makes what is going on. The UPS truck makes frequent deliveries to our house with packages for the church. This brings Dixie at the run to my feet. Without saying a word, she tells me that there is something going on which requires my attention. Like Lassie barking to the family to alert them that "Timmy is in the river," Dixie lets me know that I need to come and sign for a box being carried by a man in a brown uniform. The UPS man chuckles over the fact that he never has to ring our doorbell.

"The dog never barks," he says with a questioning look on his face.

"But she lets me know you are here," I respond. There are many ways to be a good watch dog, and thankfully, Dixie chooses the quiet one.

When either Dan or I am away, Dixie watches relentlessly. Though Dan goes to his office at the church to work nearly every day, she is equally exuberant at his return each time, as if he had been gone for months. When I have been gone to a speaking engagement, I find it strangely heartwarming to see her watching for me when I pull the car into the driveway. It is always the same ritual. She jumps from her spot on the ottoman and runs to sit expectantly at the kitchen door, which opens into the garage. The first words from our mouths when we come into the house are "Hi Dixie! How's my girl?" We stop to reach down and pat her head, and she lets us know that she has been waiting patiently and is so thankful and relieved we have returned to her safely.

When our children were teenagers they both were actively involved with our church youth group's Bible quiz team. Their quiz meets took them all over our state and sometimes to neighboring ones. Those were good times in their lives. We are so thankful that they have so much of the Bible memorized and can fall back on that knowledge when they need it. In fact, we claim the promise found in Isaiah 55:11 in which God promises that His words will not return to Him void, but will accomplish what He wants in their lives.

The quiz meets were fun for them but often became trying times in my life. The team had a player coach who was only a few years older than our children. And so, they were always going off to these quizzes, riding in cars driven by other fun-loving young people like themselves, and of course, they always stopped for snacks on the way home. I'm sure the time got away from them. What they did not know was that a worrying mother would begin to walk the hallways and watch out the windows at the time she thought appropriate for their return. The trouble was that the time I expected them was usually an hour or so before they arrived. Dan would be in bed sound asleep. I would be dressed in robe and slippers, sitting in a chair which afforded me a view of the approaching cars on our road, praying and hoping for their safe return. Like Dixie who wants to see her masters' return, I wanted my children to be home. Unlike Dixie, I did not meet them at the door. I usually just sneaked off to bed, and they never knew that I had kept a vigilant watch for their safe arrival.

When Jesus was preparing to leave the earth for His heavenly home, He told his followers they should watch for His return. In Matthew 24:42-44, He instructs them:

> So stay awake, alert. You have no idea what day your Master will show up. But you do know this: You know that if the homeowner had known what time of night the burglar would arrive, he would have been there with his dogs to prevent the break-in. Be vigilant just like that. You have no idea when the Son of Man is going to show up (The Message).

One day we heard a story that reminded us of Dixie and her smeary window. Near Libertyville,

Illinois, is the headquarters and main campus of The Lambs Farm. This organization began in 1961 as The Lambs Pet Shop in a nearby city. At its inception, there were 12 employees working in the pet shop, and all of them had developmental disabilities. It has now grown to a huge enterprise that services approximately 250 adults with disabilities every year. The people are employed to work in many different shops and have become self-sufficient in spite of their handicaps. The purpose statement of The Lamb's Farm says that they exist to empower people with developmental disabilities to lead personally fulfilling lives. Anyone who wants to receive a blessing and inspiration should visit The Lambs Farm.

My husband and I toured the farm several years ago. It was so much fun to meet the happy employees. They have few inhibitions and share stories of things they have learned while working at the farm, whether in the barns with the animals, in the restaurant, pet store, sweet shop, or bakery. One of the directors took us from building to building, telling us a bit of the history as we walked. He pointed out the homes where some of the disabled employees live in happy group settings with just enough supervision to provide for their safety, while allowing them the freedoms of people who are not disabled. Near the end of the tour, we were walking through a hallway connecting two of the buildings and were commenting on how the entire campus was spotlessly clean.

"Everywhere except here!" he nodded and pointed to a large window which was covered with fingerprints and smears. "We absolutely cannot keep our employees and residents from smearing up this glass and so we don't even try any more to keep it clean."

Those of us in the tour group waited with question marks on all our faces.

"You see," he continued, "awhile back we had a chapel service for the people here. The visiting minister preached on the words of Jesus in Matthew 24 when He tells His followers that they should always be ready for His return. He told us that Jesus would some day return to take His children home with Him and that many scholars believe that His appearing will be in the eastern sky. One of our people found out that this window faces east. Many, many times we find them clustered here with their hands and faces pressed against the glass watching the eastern sky waiting for Jesus to come and take them to their new home where they will not have any disabilities."

When I am cleaning Dixie's mess from our front picture window, I think of that other smudged window glass. And as I swipe at the glass I ask God to give me the unwavering faith of a little dog who waits patiently for her master to return—or of the folks who work at The Lambs Farm who watch faithfully for the promised return of their Savior and Lord.

16

Can I Come Up?

D ixie Lee Phillips leads a very full, happy life. She is the small queen of her domain. She romps happily through each day, playing with her bear and other toys. She goes for countless walks. She seizes every new day, knowing there will be adventures, whether they are in the form of butterflies to chase, new "people-friends" to meet, or rides in the car. While her diet is definitely predictable, her needs are filled on a daily basis. She has a warm place of refuge where she can get away from it all, and sometimes she is even allowed to sleep with her owners. She has it pretty good. In fact, if she is living a typical "dog's life," someone needs to come up with a better analogy for a sad existence.

Every single evening of her two short years in our home has ended in the exact same way for Dixie. After she has played hard, eaten and drunk her fill, and done what she needs to do outside, she comes and sits at my feet. Often I am engrossed in a television program or a book, and I don't notice her immediately. She waits patiently for a short while, but if I don't respond to her, she will place one paw on my knee. It is then that I will either pat my lap or say, "Okay."

In less than a heartbeat, I have a gray cuddle-bug on my lap. As the reader is by now aware, I have almost always had a dog in my life. Many of them have been lap sitters, but Dixie is different from all the other pets we have owned. It is not enough to her to be on my lap. She can't seem to get close enough.

The puppy book (which was long ago dropped into the trash can) said that it is impossible to maintain eye contact with a dog. "The dog cannot stand to look into your eyes and will invariably look away," it claimed. Obviously, the author of the training manual for puppies never met Dixie!

After she is told that she can come up on my lap, she places her front paws on my chest and stares into my eyes. I truly believe that if I never looked away, she would stare at me eyeball-to-eyeball, nose-to-nose until one or the other of us fell asleep. There is such depth in her eyes it sometimes almost frightens me.

As she stares at me, I sometimes wonder what she is thinking. I wonder if she is trying to tell me about her latest adventure—trying to catch snowflakes in her mouth or chasing a leaf around the yard. Or, is she trying to ask me about my day? Sometimes I can see understanding in her eyes, and I sense that she is telling me not to worry. Always I can see unconditional love in those beautiful eyes.

Having her paws on my chest gets rather uncomfortable for me in a short time, so after we have some eye-to-eye communication, I usually tell her to lie down. Sometimes she will curl into a contented heap on my lap, but more often than not, she will simply collapse with her legs in the same position, so that she is still staring at my face.

One day last week was particularly hard for me. People had said some unkind things, my mother had just been told she had a heart problem, our daughter was on the verge of losing her job, our son had a financial need, and I was struggling with the pain of tendonitis in my shoulder. When Dixie got up into my lap that night, I began to cry the tears of frustration I had so valiantly held in all day long. She licked the tears away as soon as they fell. After a while, in the gentlest movement I have ever seen her make, she quietly placed her paw on my cheek. I know that she was saying, "Don't cry. It will be okay."

Every evening since then, her routine has changed to add this new twist. After she stares into my eyes for awhile and I tell her to lie down, she very gently puts one paw on my cheek. I say something like, "It's okay Dix. I'm all right tonight." And then she pulls the paw back. Is she trying to tell me that if I need to cry she will lick the tears?

Invariably I tell her what a good little dog she is,

usually reverting to the baby talk of her puppy days. "Her is just the bestest little dog in the whole world...yes, her is!" It is then that she puts her head under my chin, cuddling exactly as a human baby would, and falls asleep. Her night time ritual is now complete.

It is at times like these that I think about my dad's homegoing. He was diagnosed with a brain tumor in July of 1987. He never came out of the hospital after his surgery. We watched him die by inches. It took over four months for his life to slip away. At his funeral our dear friend, Rev. Bill Hesse, preached from Philippians 1:21 where the apostle Paul stated: "For me to live is Christ, and to die is gain" (KJV).

Rev. Hesse said that Dad had lived his life in such a way that everyone knew that Christ was preeminent to him. And now, for Dad to die was gain—for at the moment he breathed his last breath here on earth, he breathed his first breath in heaven.

Just recently, I heard another sermon that helped me to feel better about Dad's death. This time the preacher spoke on the stoning death of the apostle, Stephen, from the biblical account found in the book of Acts. Stephen was heard to say, "I see Jesus, standing at the Father's right hand," just before he died. The preacher explained that nowhere else in scripture are we given a glimpse of Jesus in which He is standing at the Father's right hand. He is always said to be seated at the Father's right hand. The man who was speaking said that he believes when a Christian dies and goes into heaven, he is given a standing ovation by all who have traveled before him, including Jesus!

As Dixie puts her paw on my leg asking if she can come up, I often think of Dad's passing. I wonder if Dad made eye contact with Jesus and said, "Can I come up now?" And if that pastor was correct who spoke about Stephen, I think the standing ovation must have gone on for a long time.

While Dixie stares into my eyes and gently puts her paw on my cheek, I sometimes breathe a silent prayer that God will enable me to be just half the person this wonderful little dog seems to think I am. I want to live in such a way that when someday I come to the end and ask "Can I come up?" God will pat His lap. I want to climb up onto His lap, look Him straight in the eyes, snuggle under His chin, and hear Him say, "Well done, thou good and faithful servant."

When I was a young girl, a renowned scholar of Bible prophecy, Nathan Meyer, held a week long series of meetings in our church, preaching about the end times from the book of Revelation. During one of his sermons, he said that he was glad that the Bible talks about horses in heaven because he loved horses. That got me to thinking. I didn't hear much of the rest of the sermon because I was so anxious to ask Rev. Meyer a question. He encouraged questions and often said none were too trivial to ask. I suppose I was nervous as I approached him. He was a very tall man, so this little 11 year old had to tug on his coat jacket to get his attention. I remember him squatting down so he would be eye to eye with me. He took hold of one of my sweaty little palms and said, "What is it, Raelene?" (He knew my name because he had been to our home for dinner that evening.)

"Rev. Meyer, you said there will be horses in heaven—does that mean there will be dogs in heaven too?"

This wise Bible scholar hesitated for only a moment. Theologically, I don't know whether his answer was correct or not, but I know it was exactly the answer I needed to hear and one that I still hope is accurate.

"Raelene," he said with a smile, "If heaven would not be heaven for you without dogs—then yes! There *will* be dogs in heaven."

If his answer was correct, then I intend to spend eternity with Dixie Lee!

About the Author

RAELENE PHILLIPS began to write professionally in 1982, contributing short stories for children's Sunday School papers and writing for the radio ministry of the Children's Bible Hour in Grand Rapids, Michigan. She also wrote a trilogy of historical Christian romance novels—The Freedom Series—which are now back in print. Last year she completed the requirements to become a C.L.A.S.S. communicator and fulfills numerous speaking engagements.

She and her husband Dan have been married more than 34 years and have two grown children. Dan has been in full-time ministry for 22 years, and Raelene has been actively involved in the church's music, ladies ministry, and teaching.

To contact the author for speaking engagements, please write: Raelene Phillips, 1109 West Robb Avenue, Lima OH 45801.